At-Risk Students:
Feeling Their Pain, Plight and Ploys

An Open Letter to Oprah

No child abuse is more insidious and pervasive than the shame and suffering imposed on millions of school children by punitive, repeated failure and grade retention. In the mismatch between teaching and learning, the school blames the students, labels them failures, and makes failure the students' fault and problem

Unable to avoid failure, accompanying embarrassment, and pain, these deprived students resort to defensive ploys such as clowning, disrespect, apathy and hostility to avoid exposing their discomfiture. Being "bad" is preferable to being dumb. Defiance precludes exposure of incompetence. Teachers, concerned with control and instruction, treat the defense mechanisms as causes instead of symptoms, punish the offenses rather than acknowledge misbehavior as a cover-up.

Compelled to attend class, at-risk students live in fear–fear of failure, rejection, judgment, and fear of being labeled "dumb". Most of all, they fear they may *be* dumb, making defensiveness a matter of survival.

Until teachers recognize the pain, fear, and life-altering shame, they will continue contributing to the at-risk student's anguish. Tragically, students cannot help themselves. The daunting stigma of failure is tolerated only because of the faulty assumption that failing students "Ask for it." Teachers expect students to pull themselves up by their bootstraps--an impossibility--.they have no *boots*.

Unquestioned tradition and unexamined myths permit the pernicious failure and its debilitating consequences to continue. The shameful abuse needs to be brought to the attention of the public. Only through public awareness of the tragic dilemma of these suffering students with a call to action, can their imperiled lives be salvaged. Publicity, concern, and pressure can offer the helpless, hapless, innocent students the ultimate defense—exposure of their plight on the *Oprah Show*.

Thank you, Bill Page

At-Risk Students

Feeling Their Pain
Understanding Their Plight
Accepting Their Defensive Ploys

Bill Page

Bill Page
222 Wheeler Avenue
Nashville, Tennessee 37211
615-833-1086
billpage@bellsouth.net
http://www.teacherteacher.com/

Educational Dynamics Publications, Nashville, TN

1

Acknowledgments

First, to all my students, who taught me all I know about being a teacher.

To Patti, my wife of 36 years, who *knew* I would write a book *someday*, and who even after her death, continues to inspire me and give encouragement. And, to my two daughters, my three grandboys and my sister: May you find as much love and happiness in your own lives as you have brought to my life.

To my Mother, who got me when I was 6 years old and mothered me for the next 56 years of her life. Since I never knew my birth mother, she *was* my *only* mother. I never ever had occasion to refer to her as my "Stepmother."

To my friends, who expect no special mention, need no acknowledgment, and will not be disappointed when they don't get it. You know who you are—thanks for being you and for tolerating my being me. Thanks Y'all!

Published by Educational Dynamics Publishing Company
222 Wheeler Avenue, Suite 101, Nashville, TN 37211

Library of Congress Catalog Number
ISBN: 0-9773863-0-9
Printed in the United States of America

Table of Contents

Dedication

For some inexplicable reason, I began my first year of teaching without the classroom control problems I had been warned to expect and guard against. Several "do nothing" students, whose indifference to anything and everything irritated the heck out of me, quickly became my major concern and primary focus. Kenny, two years over age, defiant attitude, indifferent slouching body language, alternating between a surly sneer and a disgusted, blank look, unquestionably became my greatest "discipline" problem and my initial teaching challenge.

Kenny was king of the "not-raising-a-finger," eye-rolling, churlish group of malcontents. "I ain't doin' nothing," Kenny declared in response to my first specific, individual request for his attention, "And you can't make me." Assuming futility and avoiding confrontation, I let the incident pass, but I was unwilling to relinquish my efforts to get his participation. I continued making daily demands, requests, and admonishments. In spite of my deliberate persistence, Kenny ignored me except for an occasional grunt, sigh, or guttural sound. He flatly refused to "do anything"—even acknowledge discomfort at my being "in his face."

He Had to be a Poor Reader

Because I used personal encouragement and persistence rather than coercion and punishment, I accepted Kenny's refusal to cooperate without confrontation or putting him more on the defensive. However, teaching eighth-grade literature, I was determined all the more, to get him to participate in reading at some level. I knew he *had* to be a poor reader and I wanted a starting place for helping him. I tried cajoling, challenging, and using sarcasm, playful chiding, and humor. I offered my complete repertoire of "looks" and my own unintelligible comments and sounds to match his. I refused to give up as teachers before me had obviously done. I was just as unrelenting in my efforts to get him to make some effort, as he was uninterested in me and my concerns about his lack of cooperation and willingness to try.

Several weeks into the school year, I arranged an extended one-on-one meeting with Kenny. Eventually, in the session, gaining his trust and struggling through his defenses, I learned that he was not the poor reader I assumed him to be—he was far worse. He could not read at all! He was in fact a *non*-reader, not a poor reader. When I saw my efforts, however well intentioned, and my persistent pressure through Kenny's eyes, it stunned me. Suddenly, I felt his pain and frustration. I understood his reluctance to reveal his embarrassing inability. And most of all I recognized his apathy and defiance as defense mechanisms to be understood and respected, not to be attacked, shattered, and exposed.

Feeling Kenny's deep pain and frustration, I recalled a painful childhood incident. As I prepared to head out to do the milking, feeding, and other chores prior to eating breakfast, dressing, and walking the half mile to the bus stop, I found my large, twelve year-old bull terrier stretched-out full length against the kitchen door, preventing me from opening it. It was unusual for Pup not to be in his bed behind the stove. But, at 4:30 on a frosty morning, I was not pleased about the prospect of the morning ritual,

.and obviously neither was Pup. Impatiently, I called his name, nudged him with my foot and tried to pull the door open. Pup just lay there, eyes open, looking up at me, but refusing to get up. I didn't care that he lay there, but he was in my way. I couldn't open the door. Disappointed at his reluctance to join me or even move, I yanked the door harder, pushed Pup determinedly with my foot and yelled angrily. I knew he was awake but he refused to respond. After a number of additional commands, shouts, jerks and pokes to get him out of the way, I became irate. His perverseness, laziness, stubbornness, or whatever the heck it was, frustrated me. I wanted to punish his lethargy. Exasperated, I gave Pup a hard solid kick in his stomach. Not until that moment did I comprehend Pup *couldn't* move. I learned, subsequently, a poisonous copperhead snake had bitten Pup in the throat. He was lying by the door trying to get more air—now paralyzed.

I Understood Three Things

The sickening sensation that I can still feel in the pit of my stomach as I call to mind kicking my paralyzed dog when he was unable to move, was precisely what I felt when I realized that I was "kicking" Kenny when he was helpless to respond as I expected. When I really realized what being in my class was like and what my good intentions were like for Kenny, I understood three things clearly. First, I would not want to have me for a teacher or be in my class. Second, I, too, would probably be defiant, surly, and apathetic in similar circumstances. Third, *I* could do something about Kenny's pain, but there was nothing reasonable *he* could do that would change his plight. I changed. Never again would I "kick" Kenny or any other at-risk kid.

I dedicate this book to you, Kenny, as a way of thanking you for teaching me a valuable lesson. I would like to thank Pup, too. Pup barely survived the snakebite and eventually died at twenty-one years old, while I was away in the army. I don't know if he forgave me for deliberately hurting him—I have never forgiven myself. Thanks to you Kenny, I learned to reflect on what I could do differently and better in my teaching, rather than use my power to coerce, manipulate, and punish you and the many other struggling at-risk students I would be meeting throughout my career.

Thanks for the life-changing lesson, Kenny:

Teach

Prologue

Among the difficulties facing virtually every teacher, every day, none is more pernicious, pervasive, and persistent than teaching students whose attitude toward learning, results in frustration, disruption, and failure. Frequently labeled with names such as, "slow learners," "culturally deprived," "underachievers," "learning disabled," "troublemakers," "minimally brain-damaged," "reluctant learners," "retarded," they are most recently referred to as "at-risk." While the name derives from "at risk of dropping out," they are most "at-risk" of "not being taught." Seemingly overlooked and ignored are the misery, discrimination, and failure imposed on their already imperiled and diminished lives. Compelled to attend school where they are marginalized and stigmatized by chronic failure, the cumulative effects inevitably result in their dropping out of school after having learned very little and thus are doomed to a life-long struggle for minimal existence.

Other classroom teachers and I are not in a position to change the existing school structure underlying the bureaucratic nightmare. However, within the autonomy of our closed-door, "little corner of the world" we can at least refrain from demeaning students' lack of knowledge, while working to restore their dignity, repair some of the damage, and salvage that part of their lives they spend at school. I am convinced that teachers and other educators, given the opportunity to reflect on their beliefs, perception, understanding, and acceptance of at-risk students' misbehavior, can and will make a significant difference in the school life and learning of the millions of at-risk students suffering the indignities of chronic classroom failure.

The purpose of this book is to help teachers feel the pain, understand the plight, and accept the defensive ploys of at-risk students. As teachers acknowledge and accept the underlying causes of at-risk behaviors, they can focus on helping all students including those most at risk while improving their teaching effectiveness and building an inclusive classroom learning community, instead of focusing on the problems these students create in orderly classroom management, instructional interruptions, class discipline, and interference with other students' learning processes. These first-person, personal accounts with their unique teacher perspective offer teachers empathetic "new eyes" to see and "warm hearts" to feel the emotional tribulations of students at-risk. I hope the stories will influence teachers to consider their own attitude, examine their perception, and reflect on improving teacher-student relationships. Students, feeling more compassion and understanding will respond in kind.

Teachers often fail to recognize the embarrassment, consternation, defensiveness, and discomfiture of students at risk and thus misinterpret causal behavior. Understanding relief from boredom, cover-up strategies such as "being bad" is better than "being dumb" and recognizing that defiance of authority earns respect from peers, can give teachers new insights into at-risk student behavior, and the need for change in teaching methods. As long as teachers interpret at-risk student misbehavior as intentional or simply a poor choice, they feel justified in failing them and punishing them; but as they accept that students are constrained by lack of acceptable options, they can understand better the importance of re-visioning and revising their own teaching strategies.

React to Causes not Symptoms

Based on the premise that behavior is a manifestation of beliefs and perceptions for teachers and students alike, these first-person accounts encourage teachers to empathize with at-risk students' dilemma, while modifying their own behavior. The solution to both problems requires teachers to react to causes of student misbehavior rather than to its symptoms.

The essence of these vignettes is an appeal to teachers' emotions, perceptions, and feelings regarding their responsibility for at risk students' offensive behavior. The stories are intended help teachers take a few steps "in the students' moccasins" and offer teachers ideas, starting points, descriptions, analyses, options, procedures, examples, and suggestions for improving their students, their classrooms, and themselves.

When teachers see things differently, they behave differently. If other teachers saw what I saw, they would do what I do.

This is a "What I See" and "What I Do" book.

Meet Bill Page, A Teacher

(From an introduction by Dr. Ed Frierson)

Bill Page is a classroom teacher. For 46 years, he has patrolled the halls, responded to the bells and struggled with innovations. He has had his share of lunchroom duty, playground duty and bus duty. Bill recently finished his forty-sixth year of teaching.

He has had remarkable success in closing the gap between successful students and those at-risk. His specialty is school-alienated students, learning disabled, and those labeled troublemakers, deprived, delinquent, rebellious, and at risk. He prefers working with problem students in heterogeneous groupings in regular classes and regular schools.

Bill has spoken to hundreds of thousands of teachers in staff development programs throughout North America. He taught extension courses for twenty-six consecutive summers at the University of California at Riverside, San Diego, Irvine, Santa Barbara, and Davis, and has taught fourteen different methods courses for teachers at eighty-six universities.

As a speaker, Bill does not present himself as an "expert," instead he offers his testimonial as a classroom teacher who discovered and developed his own educational philosophy and created his own effective strategies. Bill's personal message gets at the heart of professional attitude, personal responsibility, and individual teacher initiative for increasing effectiveness and increasing the achievement of all students

Forty Years of Success

Bill Page is eminently qualified with the experience, expertise, and success to offer fresh, effective, and proven strategies that guarantee increased achievement for all students including those most at risk.

Bill served as originator, program director, teacher trainer, and demonstration teacher for Project Enable—a six-year research project of the Central Midwestern Regional Educational Laboratory (CEMREL) funded by the U.S. Office of Education. The research program, implemented in Missouri and Tennessee was replicated and jointly funded by Peabody College for Teachers and the Kennedy Child Study Center. Some of Bill's unique teaching experiences include these:

✓ Bill has run "completely individualized classrooms" going from September to June without ever addressing the entire group. And, he has done it at elementary, middle, and high school levels.

✓ He has gone for many years without giving an F to <u>any</u> student on <u>anything</u> ever and has helped other teachers to do the same.

✓ He taught a civics class of *527* ninth graders by himself in an auditorium for a year.

✓ Bill taught an individualized math class of 93 seventh graders.

✓ He taught a "wild" innovative, open school where they eliminated the walls, bells, classes, grades, report cards, textbooks, schedules, and curriculum and used a teacher-controlled, flexible schedule that changed daily.

✓ He taught in a district of 10,000 teachers and one of 300 teachers. He taught in seven districts ranging from elite to inner-city populations in seven districts in four states.

✓ He graduated eighth grade from a one-room country school with 27 kids in all eight grades.

✓ For three years Bill taught the lowest achievers in a large school in a federal research project based on the premise: "The problem isn't what's wrong with the kids, it's what teaching programs are doing to them." He taught 16 teachers to replicate the program in 8 other schools in 2 states.

✓ For 26 consecutive years, Bill has taught teachers in summer courses at the University of California to teach regular classes, to individualize, and teach students at risk by shifting their roles from taskmasters to resources.

✓ He set up and directed an innovative elementary school on an ungraded, individualized, team basis.

✓ He taught demonstration classes of "troublemakers" in a joint project for Peabody College and the Kennedy Child Study Center and Metropolitan Nashville Schools.

✓ Bill taught in a juvenile facility and psychiatric hospital.

✓ He served as a remediation specialist for two psychological services organizations.

Bill Page
222 Wheeler Avenue
Nashville, Tennessee 37211
615-833-1086
billpage@bellsouth.net
http://www.teacherteacher.com/

13

Preface

Four decades of teaching have convinced me there is a lot I don't know about children, teaching, learning, school, education, and students, particularly those students hardest to reach and teach. Using self-reflection, action research, trial and error, anxious desperation, intense concern, dumb luck, and unsolicited feedback, I discovered that at-risk students are not teaching problems, they are victims of a one-size-fits-all educational system that imposes predestined failure on them. I learned that the words at-risk refer to students at risk of not being taught.

Though I was unable to change the educational bureaucracy, I *was* able to change *me* and some of what I was doing. I developed a personal philosophy with a practical psychology by which I could teach all students including those most at risk. Of necessity, I created and used my own successful teaching strategies. I developed a long list of collateral causal teaching factors, which I do not really understand, I found, and then discarded countless unsuccessful teaching strategies.

Reducing my lists to only the absolute certainties of my beliefs, here is what I know I know about teaching.

✓ I know that teaching is an incredibly complex process involving human beings in complex interactions requiring intellectual, emotional, and attitudinal elements that defy simple definitions, applications, and explanations.

✓ I know that attempts to reduce teaching to skills, methodology, and techniques typically taught in education courses and advocated in "how-to" books is obviously absurd and when coupled with the context in which teaching-learning occurs, it is inconceivable.

✓ I know that teachers and students are the heart and soul of the educational process—they do the work of education. All others are there to support teachers in their work, not to tell them what to do.

✓ I know that teachers know their students and their classrooms. They must have the autonomy to make decisions about what goes on in those classrooms, not because they can do it best, but because they are the only ones who can do it at all.

✓ I know that children learn from varied sources, but the learning for which schools are responsible, will occur or fail to occur in the classrooms, and it will happen to each student and involve each teacher in each classroom.

✓ I know that more than classes, courses, meetings, seminars, and training sessions, teachers need discretionary time. They need time to reflect; time to dialogue with colleagues, visit schools, time to observe and work with other teachers.

✓ I know that innovation, progress, and reform are not programs to be embraced; they are at most indicators of directions which teachers must move decision-by-decision, day-by-day to maintain teaching efficacy.

✓ I know that teachers need more time to spend with individual students and families. They need time for home visits, time to spend in the library, on the Internet, reading books, journals, and more time for personal experimentation, action research, and problem solving.

✓ I know that educational change, though inevitable, is extremely difficult. Change means letting go of the familiar and grabbing on to something new and untried. Effective teachers don't resist change. What they resist and resent is "being changed."

✓ I know that the moment-by-moment, decisions I make in my classroom make a difference in the learning, the discipline, and the climate. I also know that many of my decisions are to do nothing—but they affect learning just as much.

✓ I know that I have available only 24 hours per day. Some hours (too few) go to my personal needs and endeavors, my family, and my private life. The other hours go to my teaching—to my students. I am obliged to use my precious, limited, professional time efficiently and effectively.

✓ I know that teaching, discipline, classroom management, growth, knowledge, and skills are meaningfully measured only in terms of each student's learning, achieving, and succeeding.

✓ I know that when my students figure out things on their own, when they use higher-level thinking skills, and when they have an opportunity to interact, they learn and they remember.

✓ I know that no matter how well subject matter is presented, it cannot have any effect on students until they become personally involved in the subject, content, and material in which they find personal meaning and relevance.

✓ I know that my students can only begin where they are. Their current attitude, knowledge, misconceptions, interest, beliefs, and skills, are the beginning point of their learning, understanding, and of my teaching. There is no alternative.

✓ I know that a variety of teaching techniques, strategies, and ideas are available by the thousands. It is only by focusing on the outcomes, understandings, and objectives to be achieved that I am able to select or create appropriate learning procedures and teaching strategies.

✓ I know that any school district that doesn't have discretionary cash available for teachers to buy additional materials that they need high on its list of budget priorities, doesn't really understand classroom teachers' needs.

✓ I know that genuine encouragement, personal discovery, cooperation, interaction, trial and error, self-correction, and self-improvement are the most powerful motivators teachers can use for themselves and offer to their students.

✓ I know that coercion, intimidation, reward, and punishment, however subtle, traditional, and well-intentioned, offer only temporary discipline solutions and are generally counterproductive to meaningful learning, self-actualization, and self-discipline.

✓ I know that the fill-in-the-bubble tests required by politicians at the end of the year can't possibly measure very much of what I taught in my 1,263 hours with students—certainly not important things.

✓ Most of all, I know that doing what I know for certain (devoting my professional time, energy, and efforts) makes a difference. I don't have time left for doing things I am not sure of; much less for things I know don't work. My students, my profession, and my life are too important to me to spend time and effort doing anything other than what I know I know.

As I continue reflecting, I ask myself, "How is it that I know these 'truths' while many of my colleagues wallow in their ignorance?" My only answer is, "Because I know the truth—my truth—my personally experienced truth." I am not willing to relinquish my years of learning just because others do not agree, because they learned something different, or because I am in the minority—I know I know.

Introduction

Each day, millions of students, categorized in the catchall category of "at-risk," will suffer another day of failure, embarrassment, boredom, and frustration. They will endure scowls, sighs, eye-rolling, snide remarks, and "those looks." The ill-fated students are likely to be told, shown, and reminded repeatedly that they are inadequate, incompetent, unworthy, perhaps, beyond hope. Then, the captive students will be expected to sit still, be quiet, pay attention, stay interested, participate, cooperate, like school, do homework, and behave themselves.

These *"victims-at-risk"* encounter pervasive humiliation and disapprobation. They live with failure. They feel it, hear it, see it. They experience failure in ways so subtle it is barely perceptible, to ways that are so cruel and brutal, it is inhumane. Whether emanating from school policies and assessment methods, from peer comparisons and judgments, from teacher tests, grades, and evaluations or from personal inferences, knowledge, observations, and subconscious feelings, the message is unmistakable—they *are* failures. The persistent message is pounded into their psyche class-after-class, week-after-week, month-after-month continuing for years creating a crescendo for as long as their aborted time in school lasts.

They Fear the Truth

At-risk students live in fear—fear of failure, fear of judgment, fear of rejection. Fear is omnipresent—an inescapable reality. They fear being inadequate or incompetent, embarrassed, ridiculed, or ostracized. They fear being labeled dumb. And, possibly worst of all, they fear the truth—that *they may actually be dumb*. Tormented, retained, and labeled, at-risk students pretend their failure doesn't hurt. Inevitably, they develop psychological defense mechanisms to avoid unwanted painful feelings. With their emotional survival and their very existence at stake, they desperately deny, excuse, or divert the relentless affront. Most emotions operate outside of their consciousness as they cope with the assault on their psyche, dignity, and worth.

Attention-getting behaviors of these distressed, struggling students, however disturbing to teachers and distracting to classmates, are part of what I learned as the "soggy potato chip theory." No one *prefers* soggy potato chips but if that is all that is available, people *do* eat them. Students use whatever coping strategies they can find. Negative attention is better than no attention, defiance is better than displaying incompetence, punishment is better than capitulation, and being "bad" is more socially acceptable than being dumb. Failure, apathy, and "an attitude" require little effort for them, while acting out and sassing, usually satisfying for the moment, are effective defensive maneuvers. Teachers need to recognize the ploys and gambits at-risk students use to avoid failure, deceive teachers, cover inadequacies, and rationalize their behavior. Using aggression, rebelliousness, antisocial behavior, and backtalk, students get a degree of satisfaction. By entertaining themselves and others, showing off, or proudly exhibiting a "to-hell-with-it" demeanor, they hope to improve their status among peers.

19

Students Cannot Change the Conditions

Historically, when school failed to teach children, they were given an "F" thus making the child the failure not the school. Currently, new laws, mandates, high-stakes testing, social promotion bans, and increasing societal pressure to "do something," require schools to accept more responsibility for student achievement instead of blaming the victim, ignoring the problem, or permitting dropout and dumping-ground solutions. With notoriously "fuzzy" statistics provided by schools, who knows whether conditions are improving? Certainly, whereas much needs to be learned about accepting, understanding, and teaching at-risk students, and a plethora of at-risk components creates complex issues for teaching decisions and research, the following factors serve as the basis for the "point of viewing" of the at-risk quandary:

1. After experiencing years of failure, at-risk children are not likely or perhaps not even capable of changing their attitude toward themselves, their ability, other students, subjects, teachers, and school without vigorous intervention. Students cannot change their behavior unless causal conditions and circumstances, which lie beyond their control, are changed or reduced. Schools and teachers have the obligation and opportunity to change the teaching-learning conditions capable of reversing student failure. Students have no such capability or opportunity.

2. Schools have no control of students' home life, and may not know specifically what to do to remediate students' learning deficits, but they do know many things _not_ to do. Reducing and eliminating procedures that

obviously are deleterious should be an excellent starting point. While social concerns, political action, media pressure, and public awareness highlight "troublemakers" on a daily basis, the same focus opens a window of opportunity permitting teachers and schools to acknowledge what school life is like for at-risk students and the need to re-vision what might be done to salvage their lives rather than demeaning and diminishing them. Because educators frequently misunderstand at-risk students' intentions and misinterpret their behavior, teachers are likely to ignore root causes and discriminate against at-risk students. As has been shown in racial discrimination studies, it is all too easy to discriminate against people one doesn't know, understand, relate to, or with whom one cannot empathize.

3. Teachers, as evidenced by their college degrees, have been successful in their own schooling. The system worked for them; they learned. Teachers have difficulty understanding failing students' attitudes, defenses, and actions unless it is brought meaningfully to their attention. Teachers also understand the importance of family motivation, support, and attitude. Parental involvement is not usually an option to teachers for assistance with at-risk problems.

4. The complex social structure of school marginalizes most students at risk and prevents their socializing with students who have better attitudes, better grades, better study habits, and better ways of coping with school pressure and demands. The students are limited to a circle of friends who feed off each other's bad experiences and attitude, and who are likely to sympathize with rebellious behavior and negative attitudes.

Lack of academic success increases problems with attendance, failure, and discipline. Schools pressure parents to help, but the parents of at-risk students usually have little control and frequently add to school and family alienation with increased threats. Once school and home are unpleasant or unhelpful, the people most likely to accept these troubled students are other troubled students—a prime opening for gang-type associations, drinking and drug abuse, violence, and criminal potential.

At-Risk Students—Feeling their Pain, Understanding their Plight, Accepting their Defensive Ploys presents personal experiences, emotions, analyses, descriptions, and reflections gained and gleaned through forty-plus years of teaching. By offering my personal philosophy, teaching rationale, and attitude and feelings, I want to encourage readers to consider what it might be like to be a struggling student, a failure, who is embarrassed and defensive. I want teachers to stand where I have stood, to stand where students stand right now, and feel their pain and consternation.

Teachers and students alike are victims of school's hurtful traditions, unreasonable expectations, insidious myths, and mindless bureaucratic policies. Children are compelled to come to school and teachers are required to teach predetermined lessons on a fixed schedule to everyone assigned to their class. Teachers don't have to like or agree with the bureaucratic demands; nor do they have to like or agree with at-risk students' behavior and reaction. But, through normal daily decision-making and within the autonomy of the "closed-door classroom," teachers can at least get "wiggle room" to acknowledge that students operate *only* from their own unique perspective. Teachers can begin making changes

22

accordingly and can consider and regard the students' values and background. Most of all, they can accept student's behavior as a manifestation of *their* own perceptions and offer opportunities to examine and question their point of viewing as students.

Sharing my experiences serves to remind teachers of their responsibility to teach *all* students. My descriptions remind teachers that they must begin by accepting students' current behavior. My point of viewing demonstrates there is no viable option to taking responsibility for student achievement by accepting students as they are. Teachers and students alike are "victims" of the educative process. Both groups are on the bottom rungs of the education ladder while those higher up apparently are unable or unwilling to improve the teaching-learning conditions. The crucial questions are these:

✓ Shall teachers change the way they teach at-risk students or shall they continue unsuccessfully to expect at-risk students to change themselves in order to be taught?

✓ Shall teachers wait for school reforms that have been promised but still haven't arrived?

✓ Shall the at-risk students continue to be subjected to needless pain, embarrassment, and suffering?

✓ Shall teachers exert individual effort on the students' behalf or await new policy changes?

How much longer shall they wait?

I answered these questions for myself forty-some years ago!

Addendum

There is another daunting issue of personal concern for the plight of at-risk students, but I choose not to deal with it in this book because it is an issue with which I have had limited personal experience and direct involvement, though I have certainly had maximum consternation. The unaddressed problem is the likelihood that so many at-risk students, abused by the school system's failure to teach basic literacy are, by way of alienation, peer pressure, and limited acceptable options, prone to become criminals.

I have taught students in juvenile facilities and many pre-delinquent and over-age juvenile delinquents with unbelievably long rap sheets in regular public schools. I have the same concerns any responsible member of society should have. I am well aware that *adults* rarely begin a life of crime, and I strongly suspect middle school to be a breeding ground for a number of prison-bound young people. Our approach to dealing with dropouts and at-risk students must begin before middle school and can be addressed with a simple proposition. When students come of age, if there is nothing worthwhile for them, they dropout; if there is something they can use, they stay.

In an "Essay on Equity and Justice for Diverse Children in Urban Poverty" Martin Haberman, Distinguished Professor, University of Wisconsin, Milwaukee states.

Every miseducated child represents a personal tragedy. Each will have a lifelong struggle to ever have a job that pays enough to live in a safe neighborhood, have adequate health insurance, send their own children to better schools than they went to, or have a decent retirement. In most cases their lives are limited to dead end jobs, or wasted away in street violence or prison. Miseducation is, in effect, a sentence of death carried out daily over a lifetime. It is the most powerful example I know of cruel and unusual punishment and it is exacted on children innocent of any crime. (EducationNews.org March 2003)

For the time being I will limit my presentation to the problems of at-risk students in regular schools and what classroom teachers and school administrators can do now. I shall save my concern for the ominous relationship between our failure to teach at-risk students and its causal effect on their failed lives after their failed schooling for another day.

Annotated Contents

1. Teaching: An Awesome Responsibility
I make the decisions in my classroom—all of them, always.

Whether I have a "good" class depends on me, not on my students. Whether the at-risk kids get involved, learn and enjoy my class depends on what I do. How they behave depends on how I behave. I am 100% responsible for my teaching.

2. At-Risk Students: A Point of Viewing
A summative position on the reasons and remedies for at-risk problems.

At-risk students cannot be expected to increase their achievement unless teachers improve their effectiveness. Teachers cannot improve their effectiveness unless they are willing to abandon teaching procedures that have failed and adopt strategies that take into account that at-risk students begin their schooling with different experiences and different perception of themselves, school, and the world.

3. Wealth Accounts for Achievement Gap
I respond to an Alfie Kohn Article.

"Wealth accounts for differences in test scores" so says Alfie Kohn, who goes on to show, "We've got proof." I agree and offer responses and explanations. Since poverty correlates to differences in test scores, it follows that poverty needs to be "fixed" before worrying about test scores, but schools do not have that option.

4. Take a Seat at the Bottom of the Class
But don't plan to stay too long, it will be too painful.

Fifty percent of the students in class are below average and there is a bottom ten percent in every class. Consider what it might be like for students who spend day after day at the bottom in boredom, condescension, low scores, in competition with the rest of the class, especially the top ten percent, and in fear of being ridiculed and appearing stupid.

5. "We Get What We Get"
The bottom line in parent accountability and teacher responsibility.

A blunt, undesirable, but definitive answer to the dilemma of teachers' expectation of parental cooperation in their child's schooling and the problem of parents who refuse to take responsibility for assignments, homework, and participation in their child's learning. The bottom line: Teachers must teach unconditionally—no excuses, no exceptions.

6. Successfully Teaching At-Risk Students
Understanding, accepting and repairing the damage.

An estimated twenty-five percent of children arrive at school having been reared in poverty and undesirable conditions all their lives. It is not their fault. The children were okay when they were born. They were "damaged by an adult created-managed world." The "at-risk" label is pinned on them by schools indicating they are at risk of not being taught. It is an insidious means of blaming the victim.

7. Failure Is Never an Option
The alternative to flunking students is teaching them.

Students do not just flunk—they flunk something, and the something they flunk is what I, as the teacher, am in charge of. It takes two to "Tango." You can't have a "flunkee" without having a "flunker." So long as teachers are in charge of teaching, testing, and evaluating, they choose whether students learn or flunk.

8. Discrimination against Low Achievers
Powerful, proven research that shows pervasive injustice.

A short, meaningful article from the London Times grabbed my attention and, to this day, never let go. The writer of the article asks, "How many of us really do try to give an equal chance to all members of the class?" Incredibly, a federal project modified teacher techniques so that discrimination against low achievers could be eliminated.

9. Remediation Doesn't Work
The remedial concept, not just the procedures, does not work.

If remediation works, why not take students who are behind and catch them up. Why is it schools keep remediating the same students year after year? And, they do, sometimes for their entire aborted career! If schools are still remediating them, that shows it doesn't work. In fact, if remediation works, why not use the techniques in the first place rather than after a student has encountered difficulty? Why not have all teachers use the procedures instead of just remedial teachers?

10. Teacher Characteristics for Student Achievement
Each teacher has unique characteristics.

A teacher is a human being with unique characteristics, personality, interests, differences, abilities, and knowledge. In reflecting on the three best teachers I ever had, I note that they weren't alike, they didn't have the same, or even similar, teaching characteristics; each teacher was unique. Here are three characteristics that "good teachers" possess.

11. Student Self-Concept and Achievement
Do we really believe in the importance of self-esteem?

Each day, a number of unfortunate students are told in many ways they are inadequate. The most basic elements of school structure from the lockstep grade levels, to the formal, informal, and subtle evaluations, to the competition, and constant comparisons are inescapable. Once a student hits the slippery slope toward failure, the only teachers who could help are often the ones who hasten the slide.

12. A Remarkably Successful Program for At-Risk Students
A self-contained class of the lowest achieving seventh-graders in a large school gained three to four years in achievement scores by a role reversal.

Class members, themselves poor students, became tutors helping elementary students rather than being the ones tutored. Not only does the aphorism "The best way to learn something is to teach it" applicable, but the self-concept of being "a teacher" was an obvious personal gain.

13. Murphy, the Tutor
The wondrous story of a changed life.

Murphy had been in special education in inner city St. Louis schools all his life. At 19 years old with good attendance but with no credits in high school he moved to a suburb that had no special education program. Becoming a part of an at-risk group of junior high students involved in tutoring elementary-level students. The tutoring program transformed his life.

14. Labels Are for Jelly Jars
Labels have many uses but not for pinning on students.

If a diagnosis or its label doesn't lead to remediation or isn't within the realm of one's responsibility, it becomes useless, and possibly damaging. Labels can be useful in communicating about a student, but they are useless, even detrimental, in working with a student. I've never used a label of any kind to help change a student's behavior. Instead, I use an accurate, detailed description that produces an accurate specific plan of action.

15. The Teacher Is the Difference
Many factors make a difference, but the teacher is the difference.

Whether students learn a little or a lot; whether they have a good day or bad; whether they improve their achievement depends on the teacher. Textbooks, classroom conditions, and administrative policy can make a difference, but the teacher IS the difference.

16. Kids are never NOT Learning

Only nine percent of a kid's life is spent in school, but they are always learning.

Every kid can learn is not accurate. It should read, every kid does learn. What they learn is what they experience. If they live on a farm they learn about farms; if they live in the ghetto they learn about ghettos. I've noticed that kids who come from Catholic homes are usually Catholics and those from Baptist homes are usually Baptists.

17. My Personal Teaching Credo

My credo is a public announcement and application of my beliefs

My credo serves as a summative applied part of my beliefs, experiences, knowledge, and expectations. I developed it as a statement by which all of my classroom behavior could be measured and understood. My beliefs determine my actions. Upon examining my beliefs, I then make a public commitment to my behavior as a teacher.

18. Teachers Are Individuals Too

Neither students nor teachers can be standardized.

In teacher training, they forgot to allow for individual differences in teachers. They seem to assume that all teachers have the same abilities, personalities, interpersonal skills, competencies, and teaching styles. In my twentieth year of teaching, it struck me that the school system did not regard me differently from a first year teacher. I had the same number of kids, same supervision, same preparation time, and same faculty meetings as though there was no difference.

19. Marching To a Different Paradigm

Student achievement is via teacher effectiveness.

Teacher effectiveness is through a relationship that acknowledges the independence of both the teacher and the student. Each functions independently, yet both are responsible and accountable to each other. The result of the merger of the teacher and student as autonomous learners is like a hybrid interaction and interrelation creating an Interdependent Paradigm.

20. School Learning Occurs in School

Children learn all their lives but the learning for which school is responsible, occurs in school.

Teachers don't just make a difference; they are the difference in student learning. And the keys to improving their effectiveness in increasing student achievement is first, teacher empowerment and second, embedded staff development provided by building administrators as instructional leaders.

21. My Reaction to a School Incident Reported in the St. Louis Post-Dispatch
Maybe the problems are really just symptoms.

One of every three students is absent each day, and "mobs of students in the halls being disruptive and refusing to go to class" is a problem at Vashon, an inner city high school in St. Louis, Mo. The problem made the front page, feature page, pictures, columns, editorials and letters to the editor in the newspaper. What they call problems; I call symptoms.

22. A Great Model of Differentiation
To find motivated kids, individualized learning, success with at-risk kids and differentiation too—check out the extracurricular activities.

No two students are alike, learning is personal and learning is individual—so how do teachers go about teaching lessons for a group. This chapter offers a list of the characteristics of differentiation and how it works for all students including those at-risk.

23. Fla. Tries to Avoid Flunking 50,000 Third Graders
More than 50 ideas as alternatives to flunking 50,000 third graders.

These nine-year-olds were okay when they came into the world, whatever happened to them since then is not their fault. Don't blame and punish the victim. Each child is living the only life he or she has, the least the schools could do is not diminish her life by declaring her to be a failure.

24. If You Ask the Wrong Question; You Get the Wrong Answer
The question frames the answer and so always constrains the answer.

Every question contains a set of assumptions with built-in limitations in the parameters of our thinking about the answers. Therefore, we should always "question the question before we answer the answer."

25. Kids Are Always Learning
There are seven categories of learning, which every kid experiences continuously.

All seven categories are a continuous part of every kid's learning experiences. The seven categories influence varies but it is never zero. And, it is an integral part of the school context, climate, and culture

26. Teacher Self-Reflection

I am the only one who can change me. That is not an easy task, but it can be done.

Self-reflection is the most powerful behavior changer teachers can use. It requires teachers being able to "step outside themselves"—becoming objective observers, seeing themselves from a new perspective.

27. Imposed Authority versus Natural Authority

There is a way to get a kid to sit down, shut-up, pay attention, follow directions, and want to learn; but schools still struggle with the failed stick and carrot method.

There are only two ways to control kids or make them behave—and one of them doesn't work. Schools use the one that doesn't work. If reward-punishment worked there would be no discipline problems in school, and yet discipline is still the number one problem year after year.

28. Mandating versus Teaching—People versus Products

Running schools like "bottom-line businesses" won't, and can't, work.

The analogy that equates the worker to the teacher and the product to the student is asinine. Kids are not products; they are human beings and contrary to school policies they act like humans—there's the problem. The goal is to teach students to behave, not to make them behave. That cannot be mandated.

29. Just Ask the Kids

Do students have a voice? Do they evaluate their teachers? Are they consulted?

One of the most powerful devices for gaining the cooperation of students and developing responsibility and motivation is getting the kids involved in feedback and decision making. At least they can talk about it!

30. An Afterword

Annotated References

Teaching: An Awesome Responsibility

I make decisions in my classroom,
all of them,
all of the time,
each moment,
each day,
every day.

By these decisions, I make my lessons
exciting, inviting,
stimulating, boring,
confusing, difficult, or
effective and appropriate.

My decisions establish, determine and control
the classroom climate,
the atmosphere, the aura,
the ambiance or the mood and
conditions conducive to learning

I am in charge. I am responsible for my students.
I can create anxiety,
hesitancy, uncertainty or
satisfaction, happiness,
exhilaration and anticipation.

My classroom presentations are my choices.
I have the prerogative of making them
interesting or boring,
monotonous or dynamic,
tedious or humorous,
enthusiastic or dull,.
hands-on, or lecture
participatory or passive.

My decisions, my power, my actions, my responses and
my failure to decide, to act or to respond, make my lessons
worthwhile, memorable,
worthless, harmful,
helpful, useless,
valuable, and impressive.

As teacher, I control kids' lives for a specific period of time.
I can affect and influence
their attitude,
their feelings, their emotions,
their desires, interest,
attention, thinking and aspirations.

My decisions make their lives better or worse,
for the moment,
for a little while,
for continued learning, and perhaps,
for time to come.

I remember times when I myself. as a student, felt
angry, upset, confused,
embarrassed, alone,
helpless, inadequate,
resentful and troubled.

I still harbor some of the frustration, hostility, resentment
and pain from my own school days; but
there is nothing I can do about that pain -- now.
I also recognize hurt and frustration in some of my students;

I *can* do something about their pain – now.

I can decide at any given moment
> to smile or to frown,
> to give an "F" or to give a second chance,
> to be autocratic or to be democratic,
> to be uncaring and authoritarian,
> to be caring and empathetic.
> to be contentious or contemptuous

> > My responsibility is to teach; to help my students
> > > develop positive attitudes to
> > > become confident and competent
> > > become knowledgeable,
> > > become productive and independent
> > > become world class citizens.
> > > become all they can be

Making teaching decisions is an awesome responsibility
> and the decisions
> and non-decisions
> are all mine
> all the time.
> > *That's Awesome!*

At-Risk Students: A Point of Viewing

A Position Paper

A point-of-view is how one views something; a point-of-viewing is where one stands while s/he is viewing something. I have been, (and still am), at-risk. I have stood where the troublemakers stood. I have seen the classroom from the bottom end. I have suffered failure and embarrassment. I have felt classroom discrimination, hostility and injustice. I didn't like it. It hurt. Now, here's my point of viewing.

Traditional remediation strategies for improving achievement of at-risk students have been notoriously ineffective, especially with the hardcore group at the "bottom" or with middle and secondary students who may have endured years of bad habits, bad attitude, and failure. Students who stay in school usually survive only long enough to reach dropout age whereas untold other marginalized students go through the motions of schooling with no apparent learning effect. Teaching problem learners is a daunting task. Perhaps as many as twenty-five percent of all students may be at risk, with fifteen percent qualifying as chronically failing and

35

repeating grades. Some schools may have more than fifty percent of their students in this category.

Remedial Procedures Don't Work on At-Risk Students

Remedial procedures and programs, most used and best known, include reduced ratio approaches, resource rooms, learning disabilities programs, attention deficit disorder programs, teacher aides, volunteers, alternative classes and schools, tutoring, and special homogeneous groupings. Had these procedures been effective, the at-risk problem could have been resolved long ago. NOTE: I am aware of some teachers having been successful with some seriously at-risk students, but I suspect it was the individual teacher not the program that made the difference. I posit that it was because of the teachers' personal, caring relationship and his or her ability to cause change in the students' attitude that was successful not the program content and procedures. Otherwise, the programs would have worked and still be working for most students and many teachers instead of only a few.

Traditional remedial teaching methods have emphasized changing, controlling and modifying the students' behavior rather than changing the teachers' behavior, attitude, and relationship. Because behavior is a manifestation of students' beliefs, attitudes, emotions, and experiences, it is internal and cannot be manipulated by teachers nor by their parents, who have already failed to control their children. Student beliefs,

36

attitudes, emotions, and experiences control their actions. It is their perceptions that must be examined and altered, so they can change their behavior. Such alterations and modifications can be made only by the students themselves. Because students are reluctant to take advice or counsel from anyone they don't trust, they don't like, or who has already failed to help them, it is imperative that a good student-teacher relationship be established before students can be helped to improve.

Achievement Is the Function of Choice and Commitment

Schools cannot change student behavior by compulsion, exhortation, coercion, cajoling, reward, or punishment—heaven knows they've tried! Individual student achievement is the function of choice and commitment; it is never the result of coercion. If sufficiently powerful, coercion can cause a degree of compliance or perhaps cause the students behave as though complying; but, as schools discovered long ago, coercion can also cause resistance, resentment, hostility, defiance, aggression, passive aggression, violence, subversion, vandalism, passivity, hopelessness, and a full range of notorious, disruptive, and undesirable behavior of students at-risk.

At-risk students need help seeing themselves in new and different ways, and with renewed hope and possibilities. If they perceive themselves differently, they will behave differently. I am the only one who can change me and only students can change themselves. Change must emanate from inside each individual. Perception cannot be manipulated from the outside. Through a caring relationship with mutual trust and respect, teachers can help students change their perceptions by facilitating a willingness and freedom to examine, question, compare, and consider other possibilities. Until students see themselves as capable, or until the have the desire to change, they cannot acquire the study and learning skills by which they can ultimately improve their academic achievement.

What Teachers Must Know and Do

Teachers are frequently the only adults outside of a student's family members who have the position, knowledge, and opportunity to assist students in altering their ambitions, attitudes, choices, and commitment to become more successful in school. Among factors, which teachers themselves need to consider about at-risk students' behaviors before they can begin moving toward helping those students succeed are these:

1. At-risk students are likely to have a "failure identity," which some wear like a badge of honor. By their walk, talk, dress, hairstyle, adornments, friends, vocabulary, mannerisms, and past success with their identification, they identify with other failing students and separate themselves from successful students and authority figures.

2. Most programs, reforms, and innovations have focused on changing the students instead of changing teachers' understanding of the way they need to relate to the at-risk students and deal with the problem of identity. When teachers change their approach, their responses, their

emphases and their part of the teacher-student relationship; the students can and will begin to change accordingly. It is the teacher's obligation to assume responsibility for the relationship and initiate changes.

3. In spite of the obvious, direct, profound relationship between students' attitudes toward a subject and their interest, motivation, learning, memory, and achievement, schools have not dealt with the problem of "attitude" except to mention it or condemn it. I know of no teacher who has had a course or in-service program on changing or improving student attitudes. If a student says, "I hate to write," it would be extremely difficult, probably impossible, to teach her to write, practice and improve her writing skills without changing that negative attitude first, or at least simultaneously.

4. Self-concept is crucial to school success, but self-concept is not taught directly. It is inferred by individual students. From the attitude, demeanor, and behavior of those with whom they associate and interact, at-risk students "figure out" or deduce who they are, what they are like, of what they are capable, and what they believe about themselves. Self-fulfilling prophecies, school policies, discrimination, evaluations, and assessment procedures are constant reminders providing daily reinforcement of the student's "loser" image.

5. Consistent, predictable, widespread discrimination against at-risk students is well documented and widely accepted as an existing factor. Teachers are apt to treat students with poor language skills, social

39

skills, and learning skills differently. Common characteristics of children resulting from impoverished conditions including limited and inappropriate vocabulary, clothing, hygiene, behavior, discipline and interpersonal relations, cause negative or lessened attention from teachers. Perhaps the biggest problem is that so much of the discriminatory communication is non-verbal. "Dr. Phil," a popular TV psychologist, claims that ninety-three percent of the communication in one-on-one interaction is non-verbal. Teachers most likely discriminate unintentionally, without even knowing it is occurring.

6. Students don't "spond"; they respond. In a teacher-controlled classroom, students rarely initiate behavior, but they constantly respond to teacher behaviors. As teachers change their ways of teaching, relating, or acting, toward the class as a whole and toward individual students, they find that the students likewise change. Teachers changing their own behavior, thus cause the student to change his own behavior.

Recognizing, understanding, and improving these six elements; (1) Failure identity, (2) Focus on teacher behaviors, (3) Attitude change, (4) Self-concept, (5) Non-verbal communication, and (6) 'Sponding and responding are within the purview of all classroom teachers. Unfortunately, some consider the elements to be in the affective domain, too nebulous, "feel good stuff," and outside of the behavioral objectives in daily lesson plans, so they ignore the factors that make the most difference for students at the bottom.

Keys to Success

Given these six essential factors, which teachers should understand, there are six specific, corresponding areas of change and improvement that must be considered before at-risk students will have an opportunity to achieve both academic and social success.

1. To teach at-risk students, teachers must be able to help them learn about acquiring identity characteristics and the ramifications of the choices they are making. Students need to learn that identity is a choice, which should be at a conscious level. Teachers must identify with the students and the students must perceive that they can be "like" the teacher and the good students. "If I don't want to be like you; I won't listen or accept your advice." "If I can't be like you or the good kids, why should I try?"

2. The student-teacher relationship makes the crucial difference in a student's achievement and the ability of a teacher to influence student behavior. If teachers taught better, students would learn better; if teachers taught more, students would learn more; and if teachers taught the at-risk students, the at-risk students would learn. And, it is the teacher who has the obligation and ability to improve the relationship through which students can improve their learning.

3. Research indicates two primary ways to change attitude—that is, cause a student to change his/her attitude. Both ways are crucial. First, is the teacher's attitude--if the teacher thinks the student can learn and

believes the learning to be important, the student may also believe it. Second, helping the students see themselves and the task differently— if they saw the task in a different way and saw themselves as capable, they would respond differently. Teachers could break down a task so that students see its importance, its sequential steps, and its meaningfulness, giving them the confidence that they can do it.

4. At-risk students are in the classroom grouping but not necessarily a part of the group. Teachers through their own personal degree of tolerance, rejection, and acceptance, through responses, attitude, group activities, and class lessons can and should demonstrate acceptance and understanding. Students who think they won't be accepted by a group, reject the group first. And, they will remain marginalized, unless specific teaching strategies demonstrate and encourage acceptance of all individuals by all group members.

5. The conscious awareness of possible (probable?) discrimination against at-risk students is the first step to reducing it. Safeguards such as consistent timing for responses, calling on students by random selection, class discussions, and getting to know more about the students' lives can be implemented immediately, while feedback and reflection on non-verbal aspects of interaction can be become a priority.

6. Teachers, through self-reflection, experimentation, and action research can initiate hypotheses about how their own behavior might be changed and how it might affect student behavior. Forms of providing

prestigious involvement, positive attitude, more pleasant demeanor, and improved relationship can be tried.

If Educators Can't Change Themselves, How Can they Change Students

Through many years, dropouts, force-outs, psychological dropouts, failures, over-age students, behavior problems, social misfits, and students in categories most at risk, were relegated to the lowest socioeconomic levels when they exited school, and might expect to find menial jobs and a degree of acceptance by society at that low level. But, times have changed. Society does not expect or accept failures, nor is there a place for them. Every child is expected to be a literate, productive, independent, critically thinking, self-actualizing member of society. If she is not, she becomes doomed to failure in life as well as school.

Educational excellence is achieved via instructional excellence. At-risk students cannot be expected to increase their achievement unless their teachers improve their teaching ability and effectiveness. At-risk students cannot change unless and until teachers and schools change. Certainly it's a tough job, but if professional educators can't change themselves, they should not expect inexperienced, struggling students to change by threats and exhortation or from intimidation by tests and grades.

Wealth Accounts for Achievement Gap

"Research has repeatedly found that the amount of poverty in the communities where schools are located, along with other variables having nothing to do with what happens in classrooms, accounts for the great majority of the difference in scores from one area to the next."
—Alfie Kohn, *The Case Against Standardized Testing*, Heinemann 2000.

Bill Page's Responses to Alfie's Statements

If parents do not provide the experiences that help children succeed in school, then the school must provide those experiences; not complain about what the parents did or did not do.

If we want all children to start together at the same time with the same curriculum on their first day of school, shouldn't we have "academic" entrance requirements for kindergarten?

If poverty factors correlate with differences in test scores, shouldn't we work on "fixing" poverty or compensating for its lack before we worry about test scores?

It seems to me we need to invest in pre-school and in parenting education in order to help children succeed in school, but we should not be moving the reading curriculum down—physiological readiness cannot be taught. (Contact the author for an excellent co-album on parenting called "Parenthood: The Roller Coaster of your Life.)

Let's pay high school students, who want to earn money, to go into needy homes to work with preschoolers and show parents better ways to relate. Teaching high school students the necessary skills would help prepare them for future parenthood. Two thirds of all high schools students work anyway and most of them will become parents.

As do all other children, those from impoverished homes learn too; but they learn many different things—things that the test doesn't measure. Is our goal to make all students alike?

Doesn't poverty correlate directly with parents' level of education? Perhaps it's the education level of family members that correlates that with school learning, not the poverty.

What about one-parent homes? They have less income and fewer adults to help in the education of the children or serve as models.

Students who are poor and who also don't speak English as their first language, receive a double whammy from school expectations.

Deprived and impoverished students from radically different cultures are also likely to be marginalized socially, both at school and at home, further limiting their experiences and making failure predictable.

Alfie Says, "We've Got Proof"

In a footnote (#10 on page 67) Alfie Kohn then states:

"You want proof? We've got proof. A study of math scores on the 1992 NAEP found that the combination of four variables that had nothing to do with instruction (number of parents living at home, parents' educational background, type of community [e.g. "disadvantaged urban," "extreme rural"], and the state poverty rate) explained a whooping 89 percent of the differences in state scores. In fact, one of those variables, the number of students who had one parent living at home accounted for 71 percent all by itself."

"Within states, the same pattern holds. In Massachusetts, five factors explained 90% of the variance in scores on state's MCAS exam, leading a researcher to conclude that students' performance "has almost everything to do with parental socioeconomic backgrounds and less to do with teachers, curricula, or what the children learned in the classroom."

"In Edmonton, in the Canadian Province of Alberta, socioeconomic status "was by far the strongest predictor accounting for the vast majority" of variability in grade three and grade six achievement test scores in 1996."

46

"Even a quick look at the grades given to Florida schools under that state's new rating system found that "no school where less than 10 percent of the students qualify for free lunch scored below a C, and no school where more than 80 percent of the students qualify scored above a C"

"Then there's the SAT, which, far from being a measure of merit (sometimes pointedly contrasted with affirmative action criteria), is largely a matter of family income. Break down the test takers by income, measured in $10,000 increments and without exception the scores rise with each jump in parents earnings."

Bill Page's Reaction to Kohn's Statements

My reaction to the information in Alfie Kohn's book, *The Case Against Standardized Testing*, is that it seems most reasonable and logical for family wealth to correlate with student test scores. All of my personal experiences as a student, teacher, and consultant, confirm that success in school, by every measure I know, correlates with the family wealth. Actually I have never heard any one question that idea. In fact, it is only in the past dozen years that I have heard concerns about it.

Reasons for my thinking family wealth correlates with school success:

We learn from the company we keep. And, the most significant company students keep in their early years, is their family. If those with whom we interact speak Ebonics or Italian, so do we. If we come from homes where correct grammar and good manners are used we learn correct grammar

47

and good manners. Students who read usually come from homes where reading is valued. I have observed that Baptists usually come from Baptist homes and Catholics come from Catholic homes.

What we experience is what we learn. The brain is an organ but the mind is cultural. While the experiences are complex and the result of many cultures, (e.g. southern, teenage, ethnic, class, gender) the first 5 or 6 years of their lives are primarily the result of immediate family environs. Entering kindergartners have lived and learned, in rich families, welfare families, farm families, immigrant families, large families and on and on; and they begin their schooling with that learning and knowledge. Additional knowledge is constructed on that foundation, whatever it may be.

The experiences that wealthy families can and usually provide their children are those that are most closely related to school learning and school success. A family's wealth also correlates with level of education, affluent communities, wealthy friends and relatives and a wide variety of childhood experiences. Their Children have likely been on extended, educational vacations, gone to Summer camps, taken music lessons, and had experience with computers, telescopes, video cameras, science kits, games, libraries, theater, museums, etc.

Students learn their values, mannerisms and their language from those with whom they identify. A child who speaks with a "hillbilly accent" or "cowboy twang" doesn't learn to speak like his teachers or people he watches on TV, or even the other students in his class. They

48

learn from those they want to be like, those with whom they interact and befriend, and those whom they think he can be like. Students may even make a special effort not to identify or be identified with other types. The identity includes their dress, adornments, walk, talk, interests, values, mannerisms, and language. As they start school, a child who is behind is easily discouraged. They may not attempt to compete and are likely to avoid the activities that might help them. They are likely to identify and continue to identify with failing classmates getting into a downward spiral -- "the rich get rich and the poor get poorer."

Winners in School are generally at the expense of losers. Students from wealthy families are more likely to have the confidence, the head start, the eagerness, the support, the efficacy, the resilience, the tenacity to be successful - to be a winner. The losers, those who do not see themselves in the winner category, cannot be expected to enjoy the game. Neither can they be expected to have affection for the winners or for the referees and those responsible for the school game.

Most of the extrinsic school rewards are of little motivational value to the students who fail or fall behind. Once children have a year or two of struggle in primary grades, once they feel and know for themselves they are "behind," they resign themselves to lower status and acquire a defeatist attitude. The stickers, teacher approval, honor roll, family (and extended family) encouragement, becomes less frequent, less meaningful, less sincere, less valued: even peer approval and acceptance begins to wane. Meanwhile, learning becomes more of an effort with fewer rewards and more discouragement, more negativism, more privileges withheld and more on the punishment end of the reward-punishment continuum.

Learning is constructed. New learning is associated or linked to prior learning. Since information must be meaningful to be learned, stored and retrieved, students with limited experiences, due to poverty, are not likely to have as much knowledge to build on or give relevance or association to new information. Limited vocabulary, language, skills, knowledge and social skills further impede their learning.

The Children are different. By the time most children enter kindergarten they have a vocabulary of about 10,000 words, but they are not the same 10,000 words for all of them. Combined with the slang, dialect, localisms, usage, connotations, habits, patterns, culture and the like, the differences in those from wealthy or poor families are essentially differences in language; much like one whose language is German being in Italy. Many of the kids miss out on instruction, comprehend less well, plus they tend to identify with the others who feel the same dilemma.

Summative Statement

Learning is one hundred percent cultural. What we eat, when we eat, how we eat, the utensils we use, how we sit while we eat, our manners, etc. is a matter of the culture of which we are a part. Actually, "culture" is plural, because each of us can be a part of several cultures and are a part of many sub-cultures. Our interests, skills, concepts, aspirations, experiences, values, language, manners, are learned from those around us.

Family education level and background determines living location, neighbors, conditions, and experiences. Family income severely limits the extent and scope of experiences available to the children. Statistics show that at least a fourth of all students live in families below the poverty level and through our own experiences and knowledge indicate what life is like for many students. Why would anyone question a primary, significant, crucial relationship between poverty and learning except to rationalize lack of learning as not being the education system's fault or problem?

Theodore Sizer, author of Horace's "Compromise in his 2004 book *The Red Pencil*, says:

"The best predictor of a child's educational success always has been and still is the economic and social class of his family rather than the school that he or she happens to attend. "Success," as conventionally defined and ultimately graduation thus depends largely on the chance of birth and income, embarrassing a democracy that pretends to offer equal educational opportunities for all." *The Red Pencil, Sizer, Theodore, September 2004, Yale University Press, New Haven.*

Take a Seat at the Bottom of the Class

"Don't worry, I won't keep you there long; it would be too painful."

Teachers appreciate "good" students: those who have good manners, good hygiene, good study skills, good background, good attitude, good interpersonal skills, knowledge, home support, confidence, and competence. Teachers love those who are reliable, trustworthy, alert, cheerful, attentive, able, responsive, sensitive, sensible, patient, and especially students who will do what they are told, the way they are told, when they are told, because they are told, preferably, without having to be told. And why not? Who wouldn't enjoy having "good" kids to teach?

Teachers as Good Students

Teachers themselves were probably "good" students, good enough to have graduated college. They identify with "good" students, they like their own type. After all, teachers are "their own type." We identify with people we respect, admire, and hope to emulate. We don't identify with people we don't like, don't want to be like, or don't think we can be like.

Half of All Students Below Median

Unfortunately, by definition, fifty percent of all the kids in class are below the class median and most other measures by which we compare kids. You might consider this fact next time you go to the doctor; chances are 50/50 he was in the bottom half of his or her graduating class, maybe in the bottom ten percent. How would you like to be in the bottom ten percent of a class—there is a bottom ten percent?

Would You Like to Be at the Bottom?

Consider for a moment what it's like to be a kid in the bottom of the class, or in the bottom ten percent of the class, maybe even the last one in class.

1. If becoming a better student, or even a more "acceptable" student, involved exposing your weaknesses, slowness, and inability, how much failure or risk of failure, embarrassment, or punishment would you be willing or able to take? How much motivation would it take to get you to "at least try?" How many good days might be necessary to offset the bad ones in the course of a week?

2. The kids at the bottom live with fear—fear of disapproval, fear of being judged, fear of risk, fear of being ridiculed and humiliated, worst of all, fear of appearing stupid, or worse still, actually being

53

stupid. They need freedom from fear, freedom to make mistakes, to take chances, to be willing to try, and to do it with impunity. Do they have that freedom in your class?

3. The bottom kids cannot compete with the average kids, let alone those at the top. They can't "play the school game" adequately. Players who always lose can't be expected to enjoy playing the game, work hard at getting better, or compete on a daily basis, year after year. They can't be expected to harbor affectionate feelings for the game, the other players, or the game officials. Hostility, envy, resentment, anger, dejection, or apathy are expected.

4. Kids don't learn well by having their ears talked at, by being given work that's too difficult, or by studying material that is meaningless to them. Kids don't learn from people they don't identify with, and they can't learn when they are anxious, fearful, or intimidated. Do you have students that fit this category?

5. "Good" students can accept and tolerate a degree of boredom, dull lecture, tests, grades, and stress, because there is sufficient reward, approval, support, and success. For the kids at the bottom, who get few rewards, limited approval, sporadic success, and poor grades. For those who have poor self-discipline, poor self-concept, and lack of interest, there will likely be failure, labels, punishment, condescension, and maybe pity. Kind of tough, don't you think?

The belief that there are fast students and slow students (or good and bad, smart and dumb) prevents us from understanding the real difference between the top students and the bottom students in school. Top kids are not vastly different from the ones at the bottom. The difference is akin to people speaking two different languages, say English and Dutch. The bottom kids speak a different language from kids at the top, but they are no less capable of thinking, understanding, and communicating. If you were among the bottom kids, wouldn't you be in a different circle of friends, speak from a different perspective, and have experiences different from the students in the top half of the class?

Studies show that when top students get low test grades it can be expected to encourage them to renew their efforts and study harder. But when poor students get low grades, it causes them to give up trying and working, figuring it won't do any good to try again or work harder. Low grades simply confirm their failure attitude. Provisional grades, retake opportunities, and practice tests—which are considered diagnostic—are of little value to high-scoring students, but could make a difference in both attitude and performance of struggling students. Are you giving the low-performing students encouragement of a second chance or opportunity to improve?

Consider the following questions from the perspective of a low-performing student.

✓ Would you resent or envy those for whom school is enjoyable?
✓ Would you blame others or yourself for your plight?
✓ Would you strive to "make" the honor roll?
✓ Would you identify with the good kids, or they with you?
✓ Would you keep trying after a failing grade seems inevitable?

✓ Would you end each school day with very different experiences?

✓ Would you at least do the part of the schoolwork you could do?

✓ Wouldn't you seek ways to make the hurt or pain go away?

✓ Wouldn't your attitude be adversely affected?

✓ Wouldn't you daydream, let your mind wander, stare out the window?

✓ Wouldn't you welcome distractions, and create a few of your own?

✓ Wouldn't you be drawn to other students in similar circumstances?

✓ Wouldn't you rationalize, generalize, and project your problems?

✓ Wouldn't you "live" with your problems every day of your life?

✓ Wouldn't you deal with boredom by "entertaining" yourself and others?

What Makes the Most Difference in Your Life as a Learner?

If what we learn is what we experience, if we learn from the company we keep, and if acceptance and self-worth are high on the list of personal needs, what would we, as low-performing students, be learning in school each day or over a long period of time? And, if the experiences and learning is not what it should be, who has the obligation to make a change in what is happening? Must the kid change before we can teach him/her, or must we change in order to teach him/her?

My Own Consideration

For many and varied reasons, school is inappropriate for a significant number of students, particularly those at the bottom. And when it is inappropriate, students act as though it is inappropriate. They act as anyone might act when confronted with impossible, boring, irrelevant, incomprehensible tasks. Teachers, in turn, act as though there is something wrong with the students rather than examine inappropriate material or our part in the problem. In my opinion, any given kid at the bottom is a prime example of this consideration. There is nothing the kid can do about it—but there is something we as school people can do.

Kids Can't *Be* Different; They Can *Become* Different

Kids are living the only life they have—the only life they will ever have. We cannot change their past. They have the parents they have, the language, the learning, the study skills, the experiences, and the interests they have. They have the attitudes, knowledge, habits, confidence, and self-concept they have—and they cannot be different. But they can become different. To become different they must see improvement as a viable alternative and be able to move one step at a time. The act of becoming is a process that requires a reason to hope or believe and a systematic procedure to bring about change. The least we can do is not demean their lives with our evaluation procedures. We can at least begin to help them to become the people we would like to see them become. And we can begin now, each teacher in each classroom with each kid.

Kids cannot be different from who they are; but with our help, they can become different.

"We Get What We Get": The Bottom Line In Parent Accountability

Following is a somewhat blunt, but quite definitive answer to the questions so often asked by frustrated teachers:

"What is the parent's accountability in their children's education?"

"What do teachers have the right to require and/or expect from parents in the way of participation in their child's learning?"

"If the parents won't see that their child gets his assignments done and won't come to conferences, what can the teacher do?"

"THE" ANSWER

Whether students have four, two, one or no parents;
Whether they are reared by grandparents, relatives, or by *others*,

Whether they have 16 brothers, plus halves and live-in cousins;

Whether they live in a house, apartment, project, or mini-van;

Whether they have clean clothes, good hygiene, and good manners;

Whether they speak English, sign language, or a foreign language;

Whether they are challenged physically, socially, or mentally;

Whether they have good interpersonal skills or study skills;

Whether they are underachievers, over achievers or non-achievers;

Whether their personality, character, and religion are to our liking;

Whether their parents are literate, retarded or English speaking;

It makes no difference to educators.

Given laws of the universe (over which we have no control);

Given students' inalienable rights (after all, you can't shoot them);

Given a hierarchy of government – from federal to local;

Given the laws and bureaucracies, governing education;

Given rules, policies, procedures, traditions, history, etc;

It can all be summed up in five words:

We get what we get!

Parents get the kids they get.

Kids get the parents they get,

(Or the life they get without parents)

School districts get the families they get.

Individual schools get the families they get.

Teachers get the students they get. And

Students get the teachers they get.

The way it is, is the way it is.

Everyone involved works within the parameters

of the laws, rules, and responsibilities; and even

within what happens outside of those parameters:

Indeed,   "We *do* get what we get."

We accept our kids. We accept the responsibility.

We take them as we find them and develop their potential,

We teach them what they need --

What we want them to have and to know.

We use whatever resources we have or can find.

We develop or create what we need.

 If the parents are good resources, we use them.

 If they are not, we do it without them.

Within the politics, mandates, mission, goals, strategic planning,

curriculum, and educational policies, we take kids where they are and we teach them. We teach them whatever is required by those rules and within that structure.

We Teach Unconditionally—No Excuses, No Exceptions

If they lack manners, we teach them manners;

If they lack study skills and prerequisite knowledge, or

Interpersonal skills, we teach them what they lack.

If they lack home resources, materials or breakfast, we provide it.

If they lack adequate visual and auditory or physical capability, we compensate.

If they don't *fit* our structure, we change to accommodate them.

We offer alternative methods and procedures.

Our job is to teach the kids we have!

Our job is to teach the kids we have.

Not the kids we used to have;

Not the kids we would like to have;

Not the kids we dream about;

Not the kids who were like us when we were students;

Not the kids who wear clean clothes;

Not the kids who are respectful;

Not the kids who speak English.

Our job is to teach the kids we have – each and every one.

Not just the kids who have responsible parents;

The bottom line: "We get what we get!"

It is natural for teachers who, themselves, have probably had parental support in school all the way through college, to see that their students would learn if they had parents to help, supervise and tutor their kids, but to force the issue of parental help after a certain point is futile. Our energies should be spent helping kids rather than worrying about parents who have shown they are of little help.

Actually, there is a bottom line to the bottom line:

Each kid is living the only life s/he has -- the only life s/he will ever have. The least we could do is not demean it, not relegate him/her to marginal status, not beat him/her over the head with his/her weakness and past history. We could accept him/her unconditionally and teach him/her whatever s/he lacks. Is there a viable alternative? Are we not capable of teaching kids what they need to know or do?

Successfully Teaching At-Risk Students:
Understanding, Accepting, and
Repairing the Damage

*Teachers and schools can rescue children with damaged
lives instead of diminishing their lives by continuing their
failures.*

Damaged by limited experiences in the child-rearing process, children labeled at-risk become the responsibility of the educational system. While the label indicates that the child is at risk of failing; it more accurately describes the school's unwillingness or inability to respond adequately to the child's limited background and inability to profit from the lock-step, age-grouped, fixed curriculum, that awaits initial school entrance.

At-Risk Children Have Been "Damaged"

"Damaged," applied to children seems harsh, but unfortunately, through no fault of their own, many children grow up with deplorable poverty, poor parenting, cultural disadvantage, language differences and experiential deprivation. It is not their fault; they were okay when they arrived. However obvious the damage and whatever the precipitating causes, schools must not wait for the higher-up bureaucrats and politicos to direct them to salvage the children's damaged lives, or to teach them how to do it. Tomorrow, these precious, vulnerable, innocent children will present themselves to school as mandated. With an age cut-off, the most children can do is "show up." Whatever the students background, schools and teachers can do more – they can teach the students who show up!

The Problems and Effects Are Well Known

The life-long consequences of an inadequate education are well known. At least one-fourth of all students are affected by lack of success. School failure is associated with illiteracy, unemployment, substance abuse, incarceration, babies born to young teens, welfare lives, abject poverty and a likely continuation of the poverty cycle.

Schools are not responsible for poverty, parenting, cultural differences and early childhood learning or their subsequent effects, but in the mandatory educative process, there is opportunity and obligation to salvage these young lives. Labeling children "at-risk" makes it appear that the children create the problem when, clearly, the problem arises because of the attitude, approach, procedures and ineffectiveness of the school system.

Which Students Are At Risk?

Students with mostly failing grades, who have been retained in grade or those who are frequently absent and who are likely to drop out, are at-risk. Students with families below the poverty level and who move often are at-risk. Additionally, at-risk students include those who have parents and siblings with poor attitudes towards school as well as those who have ethnic and cultural differences. Given the adverse prior conditions to which students are exposed and the one-size-fits-all curriculum, to which they are subjected, their failures could have been predicted before they were born.

At Least We Should Avoid Contributing to the Problem

Children at-risk are living their lives according to their experiences. It is the only life they have; the only life they will ever have. Children must not be blamed for the damage done to them in the process of living and growing in an adult-managed world. They did not choose their learning, their lives or their life style, nor did they choose to be learning problems. The least the school could do is to not denigrate their lives by labeling them failures and allowing them to be poorly educated.

These kids were not failures until they came to school. It is school and school alone that marks them as failures. School stigmatizes them with permanent records, comparisons, condemnation, condescension, marginalization, retention, and discrimination. School is not responsible for children's prior learning but they could avoid contributing to the damage.

The First Step is Understanding and Accepting the Children

Educators can begin the salvaging process by understanding the student's plight, and accepting students "as they are". Why should a child begging for attention, acceptance, recognition and belonging in the only ways s/he knows be rejected, punished, ostracized and regarded a behavior problem. They have just one problem – they are human beings. They have the same hierarchy of needs other humans have. They defend themselves and their egos when threatened. Would you have been different than they, if you had been reared in their family?

Examining Our Expectations

Teachers need to examine their expectations. Do they believe in encouragement? In a good self-concept? Do they really believe that, exhortation, negative reactions, failure, disparaging looks, derogatory comments and punishment are good ways to help the kids change their behavior? Doesn't it seem strange that professional teachers have difficulty changing their own behavior even enough to accept that children can't change their behavior totally? Should they not make a distinction between teaching children to behave and making them behave?

Beginning with "A Failure Identity"

By their walk, talk, dress, hairstyle, friends and mannerisms, the lowest achieving students exhibit a failure identity. It is their identity that must be addressed. Failing students become members of a sub-culture of students who sometimes openly express disrespect, disregard, and disdain for school. Attempts to change their knowledge and achievement ignore the basis of their behavior. Their behavior identifies who they are; it stems from their need to be accepted and their emotional survival skills.

To change identity, students must have a viable alternative to failure, be aware of problems associated with that identity and see positive value in acquiring a different identity. Students can learn a new identity through new associations, models, and experiences. It requires better understandings and relationships with those whom they desire to be like. Teachers are usually the second most important person in influencing a young child's life. They have the best opportunity to intervene, relate, change student attitudes and help the child develop new competencies

Belonging to A Group or Sub-culture

Speaking mannerisms frequently identify individuals as belonging to certain cultural, ethnic or socioeconomic groups. Consider sub-cultures who speak like a "hillbilly", like an "English butler" or like a "valley girl". People judge others and readily categorize them according to their speaking style, dialects, vocabulary, interests and behavior. Think about movies characterizing wealthy celebrities, homeless people, biker gangs, or high school cliques by their language.

Failing students befriend other failing students. They find satisfaction in wearing their failure and low social status proudly like a badge of honor. Expelled from school for behavior problems, a student enrolling in a new school will immediately team up with what he thinks is the worst child at the new school. Each knows the many identifying characteristics well. Their identity can be a source of pride and power – it is their personality.

A Matter of "Life and Death"

For the most impoverished at-risk children, success can be a matter of "life and death". Failure to "make it" in school may leave them without hope. They are not likely to have the family resources, connections, or associations to compensate for failure. Without adequate living and job skills, they are probably doomed to continue lives of abject poverty, association with people frequently in trouble and in conditions of desperate existence, poor relationships, self-destructive living styles, violence, inadequate health care, and immobility. Education is their best and last hope.

Intimidation and Coercion Have Already Failed

Persistent failure causes students to stop trying or caring. Repeated failure causes parents and teachers to stop trying to motivate children except by additional coercion, which has already failed. Individual achievement is never the result of coercion. Coercion can cause compliance but it can also cause resistance, resentment, hostility, antagonism, defiance, aggression, and apathy. When at-risk children see themselves as failures, no amount of continuing failure, compulsion, intimidation, cajoling or bribery will change them.

Identity Is The Problem

For at-risk students to succeed academically, they must see themselves as capable of succeeding, and they must desire to do so. Many at-risk children gave up long ago on both counts. Seeing the behavior of low-achieving students as manifestations of beliefs, attitudes, associations and experiences, classroom teachers can help students see themselves differently. The change in perception can be accomplished through a trusting, caring, accepting relationship. Knowing self-esteem is inferred, teachers must act to help children "figure out" they are capable.

Approach To Repairing the Damage

Traditional remedial approaches for dealing with at-risk children, especially hard-core, lowest achieving students are notoriously ineffective. If it were effective the problem would have been eliminated. The years of damage to emotions, feelings and attitudes must be repaired. Following are six important considerations for repairing the damage. .

1. A teacher-student relationship of mutual trust and respect is crucial. Teachers must empathize with these students and take the initiative and responsibility for improving the relationship.
   a. The children must perceive they can be like the teacher, and like the successful students.
   b. If students believe teachers have their interest at heart, they can accept help and advice.
2. Attitude is over-riding. If a child says, "I hate math!" or "I hate this stupid school!" That is an attitude. If teachers can't change the students' attitude, they can't teach them. Research shows two ways to help a child change his/her attitude:
   a. By teacher's own attitude, students know whether their teacher thinks they can succeed. Students spend many hours "learning" their teachers. They know their teacher's attitudes, beliefs and values.
   b. By helping children see the situation differently. If children perceive differently, they will behave differently. If they saw what teachers saw they would

70

behave as the teacher behaves or recommends.

3. Responsibility is a critical key to self-esteem: the key to responsibility is participation. But students cannot be responsible for anything in which they have no part or no voice. At-risk students must have the opportunity and encouragement to participate.

   a. An outstanding characteristic of at-risk children is that they feel no responsibility for what happens to them. They are likely to see themselves as victims – helpless, hapless dupes. Until they begin to participate in factors that affect their lives, they cannot change. Teachers cannot "give" responsibility, but they can offer and promote participation.

   b. Students learn what they experience. If they live on a ranch, they learn about horses. If they live among people who use profanity, they use profanity – children learn what they live. The question teachers need to ask is, "What experiences might I offer to help the child learn skills and behaviors toward a new identity."

4. Students learn from the company they keep. At-risk children may be in the class physically, but they are not part of the group. To become a part of the classroom community, there are four requirements.

   a. The group and its activities must be inviting. Children must want to join. They can be compelled to be in the group but not a part of the group

71

b. b. The organization must accept people "like them" – they must identify with members of the group and share its goals.

c. If at-risk children expect to be excluded they avoid rejection by rejecting the group first.

d. If joining the classroom community means rejecting other groups that their friends and family belong to – they won't join.

5. Tests, grades and report cards are the schools' ultimate, public, definitive, irrefutable rejection. For children at-risk to see themselves as capable, the assessment system and policies must be changed or eliminated.

a. The most unfair classroom procedure in school is treating every student alike. There is nothing more unfair than the equal treatment of un-equals. To give children who are different the same test after the same exposure, to the same material at the same time is blatantly unfair.

b. The goal of school is learning. Testing is learning; a 70 on a test means the student needs to learn 30% more – not get a "D."

c. Marks should never be made on a student's paper (for others to see). Post-it notes, other paper (a letter) with positive remarks.

d. Use tests for showing the children the goal. Let students take the test several times the way states do for the drivers' license exam.

e. Make testing time flexible. Give the test orally if test answers have been memorized.

6. Use a meaningful assessment procedure that won't hurt or embarrass students. At-Risk children don't need grades; they need to be taught. Failure must not be used as a replacement for learning and teaching.

   a. Assessment normally consists of three elements: measurement, evaluation and symbol for evaluation, e.g. Measurement: That apple is big as a basketball. Evaluation: Wow! Symbol: Super-dooper Humongous or SDH or A++++.

   b. Measurement: He got one of ten division problems right.

   c. Evaluation: Apparently she doesn't understand the process.

   d. He needs to review previous lessons. Grade is unnecessary. Letter symbol is for reporting the evaluation to others. Only the child and those working with him/her for improvement need to know so they can help, not so they can judge.

Pygmalion in the Classroom

The potential of the Pygmalion effect is virtually unquestioned. Teachers' expectations influence student performance and as humans, teachers discriminate on the basis of their expectations or biases, however unintentionally. The behavior of teachers change depending on their perception of whether the student is "good" or "bad". For example, facial expressions—a smile for the good student, a frown for the bad one, even discrimination in the amount of time teachers allow for the students to answer a question has been documented repeatedly. Sometimes, teachers demand levels of performance that are simply impossible for the struggling student to achieve because the student doesn't have the prior learning skills necessary to master a new task.

Lack of Learning Is Cumulative

Once a student begins the school year already behind classmates, the learning deficit accumulates and increases. Students behind one year in first grade arithmetic or reading will not be one year behind in eighth grade; they could be eight years behind. Slow learning is often a matter of coming to a task without the prerequisite knowledge to do that task. The learner needs to be taught the prerequisite knowledge. But it is not that simple. The at-risk student has been "provided" that knowledge many times before and thinks "I can't do that." That is why attitudes must be changed.

Remediation Is Not a Remedy

If a student does not know the multiplication tables in eighth grade, after having been "taught" those tables through several successive years, another go-round of remediation becomes futile. Worse than futile, because when it fails again, the notion of failure becomes further ingrained. Teachers frown, get frustrated, and finally give up. If they give up on students, why shouldn't students give up on themselves? Finally, because failure is difficult to admit to oneself, the students do some mental gymnastics and become more convinced that they hate math, the teacher and school.

Rather than beginning with remediation, teachers need, we need to begin with those behaviors and characteristics that enable them to readily recognize at-risk characteristics. Then, by teaching student self-reflection techniques, they can increase the student's awareness of those identifying characteristics. Aspects of student self-reflection include thoughtfulness about current behavior, deliberation among possible choices of alternative behavior, and reflecting on a series of actions in effort to consider a new course of action. To engage in self-reflection, the student must feel secure, be willing to take a risk, and have the opportunity to try again and reflect again.

Aspects of the reflection process includes dialog, facilitation of the process, student's desire and need to improve strengths and weaknesses. Once students are aware of factors causing undesirable results, they can process new information and accept feedback. Without awareness of need, there can be no change.

Self-Concept Is Inferred Not Conferred

At the outset, the student must be involved in all phases of the evaluation process. Involvement gives the children an interest, a stake in the process. Student involvement includes participation in task analyses, grading their own papers, student-led conferences, a personal portfolio maintained and managed by the child, participation in testing, correcting, reviewing, recording and reporting. Self-worth is *inferred;* students need to figure out things for themselves.

Relationship of Learning and Goals

Teachers can offer diagnostic or trial tests in lieu of evaluative or recorded tests. They can shorten tests by offering five spelling words at a time rather than twenty. A ten-question test can be offered in two parts, or written work can be judged by content without grading context. All of this is towards self-confidence and improved attitude.

Students must see a direct relationship between learning goals and learning procedures and assessment. Teachers can help students begin judging themselves by their personal best achievement rather than comparing to others. Students can learn "temporary failure" as a part of learning, not as a determination of worth. They can profit by feedback and understand that false progress based on cheating or charity is detrimental now and for their future progress.

Principal's Can Be the Key to Success

Administrators are responsible for teacher morale in working with the at-risk student. Principals should help teachers develop and use specific techniques such as "authentic learning", the project approach and thematic concepts as a part of educational policy. Principals should see themselves and their policies as resources for teachers in the same way that teachers become resources for their students rather than taskmasters. Focus is on helping individuals, teams and study groups through embedded staff development efforts.

Of course, principals must build a school learning community to help teachers build classroom learning communities. Whatever principals expect teachers to do with students is precisely what principals should do with teachers. If they want teachers to allow for differences in students then principals should allow for differences in teachers. With everyone working together on behalf of the at-risk students, they will have an excellent chance of making the grade.

Failure Is Never An Option

One of the most profound turning points in my teaching career came about when I really understood that "Failure should never be an option in any classroom!" If we are going to have mandatory attendance, we must have mandatory teaching. We can't command kids to come and then flunk them. The alternative to flunking kids is not passing them—it's teaching them.

Kids do not flunk! They cannot flunk! No kid on this earth has ever flunked –they get flunked. It takes two to "tango." You can't have a "flunkee" without a "flunker". Kids do not just flunk. They flunk something. And, the something they flunk is that for which I as the teacher am responsible. My classroom, my teaching, and my life were irrevocably changed with the realization that failure is never an option.

Kids don't flunk, they flunk what I teach, the way I teach it; with the information I give, the way I give it; with what I say, or fail to say; with the examples I use, with the vocabulary I use, with the experiences I plan, with the time I allocate; with which kids I call on, with the assignments I give, the discussions I lead, with the activities I offer, with where I begin, with the review I give, with the feedback I give, the practice I assign and the evaluations I make. My teaching decisions, determine what my students learn and whether or not they learn.

Teachers Determine Testing Procedures

Furthermore, they don't just flunk what I teach and how I teach; they flunk the tests that I create, the type of questions I choose, within the complexity or difficulty I choose, within the time limit I set, with the testing procedures, test item wording and variety and conditions I set, with the scoring and grading system I choose, whether "spelling counts,"(Including whether I taught the spelling or just counted it.), whether partial credit is permitted, whether I prepared all students adequately, whether it requires memorization, understanding or analysis, whether I taught them all by way of the same lessons or whether I differentiated and individualized.

Any testing condition I declare or modify, changes the score. If I offer a "bonus" question, extra credit, collaboration, use of notes, extra points, or declare that question number six doesn't count. If I had taught it better they would have learned it better: If I taught more they would have learned more; if I had taught twice as much they would have learned twice as much; if I had taught it thoroughly they would have learned it thoroughly. If I had taught each and every child, each and every one would have learned. We cannot separate our teaching from their learning. And, if I'm making most of the decisions, their learning is not a 50–50 arrangement.

Grades Are Subjective

In short, what they learn is what I teach, and what they score is what I test. The grades are totally subjective because my teaching reflects me. If I teach it, it reflects my decisions, emphasis, attitude, values, beliefs, and emotions. Even with an objective test, tests don't test kids, I test kids because I determine the test. The test is 100% my choice. I choose what to teach how to teach it; and what to test, how to test it, and how to score and mark it. You can't get any more subjective than that, no matter how "objective" the questions or how standardized the testing conditions.

Many, Many Variables

All of these considerations added to the averaging and combining procedures, make the grading process even more subjective. If I average the scores at the semester for a kid and he gets a "D," I could have probably changed that grade, just by having eliminated some of the test questions or adding some questions; or adding a test or taking away a test, or giving 10% for class participation. Would it have made a difference, if I had given a "practice" test or an extra day of discussion, or pop quizzes, preparation quizzes or study guides; or if I had used hands-on activities, small cooperative groups to review or help one another; or used peer tutoring; or given better review, discussion, or questioning exercises?

The Meaning of Grades

Have you ever had a kid at the semester, miss a "C" by seven-tenths of a point? Seven-tenths of a point on a half a year's work? Are your tests so valid that a fraction of a point is the difference in failing and passing or getting a "C" or a "D"? How would you like to submit your tests to a testing authority, or even to me for evaluation of reliability, clarity, fairness, or validity before giving them? Have you ever put a trick question on a test? Or given "bonus points?" Why?

Have you ever had a kid miss the last third of the test because he ran out of time? Did the "F" mean he didn't know the material, or that he read or worked too slowly? Have you ever thrown away a test of a kid who was talking or turning around in her seat? Was the "F" she got because she violated a rule or she didn't know his math. If the "F" was in math, will one who looks at the grade next year know that she knew the math, but didn't know to follow correct testing procedures? Have you ever lowered a grade because the paper was turned in late? Does that grade represent her learning or her ability to get work done on time?

Have you ever returned marked test papers, and had a kid say, "But, Mr. Page, I knew number 5, I thought:" "Too late?" Too late for what? If she can show she knows the answer but was confused by the question, why can't she have credit for it? The reason is usually our notion of fairness or of standardization. Neither of which is appropriate because our concern should be for whether she has learned what she is supposed to know. If she can show she knows it, she should get credit for it. Learning to work faster, follow procedures, or turn work in on time are different lessons requiring different teaching and different criteria. Are we obligated to teach it or just test it?

My Purpose for Tests

Why can't a kid take a test to see if he knows the material? If he doesn't know the material, he can study the material, retake the test to see what he still doesn't know so he can study some more and take the test to show that he has learned it. Why can't I give the test so I can determine whom I have taught and whom I have not? If I find that some students didn't learn, I can use that information to reteach. Why can't I use the test to determine how I am doing; or know which kids I need to offer something more or something different?

For me, grading is as simple as this: once it became my goal to make sure kids learn, I quit doing all the asinine stuff teachers had done to me as a student in the name of grading, especially in college, all in the name of competition, control, discipline, and the fairness of competing for grades—not for learning (see Afterword for tips on how I accomplished this in today's regulated atmosphere).

Discrimination Against Low Achievers

The following is an excerpt from an article by Stuart Smith, which appeared in the Educational Supplement, of the *London Times*, entitled "Tackling Disadvantages."

A great deal of current research indicates that many teachers positively discriminate against students they perceive as low achievers. In four different unrelated studies, the following facts were revealed:

A. The teachers give the high achiever approximately five seconds to answer question; whereas, the low achiever gets approximately two seconds to answer the same type of question.

B. Low achievers were far more likely to receive a derogatory remark from the teacher for answering incorrectly or failing to answer.

C. The low achiever received less praise than did the high achiever when they knew the correct answer.

D. When the high achiever experienced difficulty, the teacher repeated or rephrased the question 67 percent of the time, whereas the low achiever received such help 38 percent of the time.

Discrimination against low achievers was found in every single classroom observation made in both England and the United States. The author's view, based on a large number of classroom observations in Britain, the United States, and Canada, is that many secondary school teachers in oral work largely ignore those students whom they perceive as low achievers. The author placed himself in this category. The author concludes the article by asking, "How many of us really do try to give an equal chance to all members of the class?'"

In an attempt to break the pattern, Sam Keyman, a Los Angeles researcher with the California Office of Education, developed a teacher in-service training program for teachers titled "Equal Opportunity in the Classroom." This project was funded under a federal grant and continues to this day. The project seeks to modify teacher techniques and so that discrimination against "low achievers" would be eliminated.

Should you wish to experiment for yourself participating in the in-service program, select five "target" students in one or more of your classes for whom you hold high expectations, and five for whom your expectations are low. Then, once every two weeks for three months, another faculty member should observe you. Each observation takes thirty minutes. The observer will code the frequency with which various teaching behaviors are directed toward the students with the high and low expectations.

Many secondary school teachers testified that after following the above program, they increased student self-confidence and improved their classroom teaching. They also spoke of having established a better classroom atmosphere with fewer discipline problems, and improved teacher-student relationships.

In conclusion, the author indicated Kerman's work is respected among California teachers and it is widely believed, he made an important contribution to tackling the problem of underachievement in our secondary schools. Stuart Smith is deputy head of Stamford County Second Schools, Tameside.

A Bill Page Addendum

Just the awareness of a problem's existence or its potential to exist can be reduced by a periodic reminder of the extent of the problem. Some useful gimmicks you can use to reduce many biases described above are these:

1. Use a cup filled with Popsicle sticks on which class member's names are written to choose names randomly (and fairly) as you ask questions. You can substitute index cards with each student's name, shuffled, cut selected from the cards at random by students who randomly select the sticks or cards.

2. Use a check-off list on a class roster to ensure that every student is called on over the course of a day or two of discussion

3. A designated student with a stopwatch might ensure a five second wait interval between asking a question and calling on a student.

4. Groups of three or four students might discuss questions and take turns in giving s response from the group.

5. When a student answers a question, she goes to the rear of that row and everyone moves forward. Over a period of time, everyone will be in a front seat or, at least a different seat, changing the usual pattern.

6. Share the problem of bias so that the students can be aware of it and the fact that you want help. When you turn students loose to solve the problem, there will likely be no problem left to solve.

7. Use various non-verbal signals instead of hand-raising for students to let you know they want to answer. Hands should be held close to the chest so only the teacher can see the signal. For example,

   a. Thumbs up; thumbs down.

   b. Colored palm-held cards that signal, "Know," "Don't Know," "Confused" or "I have a question."

   c. Hands raised with one two or three fingers or fist.

   d. Hands held under the chin for finger signals.

   e. Arms crossed over chest.

Remediation Doesn't Work

If remediation works, why don't we take all of the kids who are behind, catch them up and be done with it! Why continue to remediate the same kids year after year? It's because: REMEDIATION DOES NOT WORK!

The remedial concept does not work—at all—for anyone, ever! The concept, not just the procedure, does not work. It is not a matter of which remedial program or process is used, or which teacher uses it—remediation simply does not work! In fact, if the remedial concept works, why don't we remediate those who are behind, catch everyone up, and eliminate the problem? If remedial procedures work so well, why don't we use those procedures in the first place instead of after students have already failed to learn? If remediation works, why don't we have all teachers using the techniques instead of special or designated teachers?

The Premise is Wrong

Remediation is essentially based on a premise of "more of the same." If they can't read, give them more reading. If they can't spell, give them more spelling. If they can't do math, give them more math. Take it slower, make it simpler, do it in smaller chunks, do it one-on-one, offer them M & M's, but keep shoving the same stuff down their throat. While that sounds perfectly logical, it is the same as saying if they can't swim, throw them into the water twice as often because they need it twice as badly. If that isn't sufficient, let their mother throw them in for a couple of hours each night at home; hire a swimming tutor; send them to the resource pool, send them to the university swim clinic on Saturday, and fill their Summers with yet more of the same. Some kids have been in remediation their entire school lives. If we know how to remediate learning deficits, why don't we do it? Why would we not have worked ourselves out of a job long ago? If we are still remediating them, it shows clearly that it isn't working.

You Have To Change Their Attitude

There is only one way you can teach kids to swim, if students are two years past the time they should have leaned to swim. If they are just learning, there are many ways to teach them or more accurately, for them to learn. But, if their friends have all learned; if they feel stupid because they can't swim. If they have been trying for a long time with no success, there is only one way you can teach them to swim, and I can guarantee it. YOU HAVE TO CHANGE THEIR ATTITUDE!

If you can't cause them to change their attitude, you can't teach them! If you can't change their attitude toward swimming, their attitude toward their own capability of swimming, their attitude toward water, their attitude toward the need to swim, and their attitude toward you, they will not learn to swim. If you can change their attitude, you can teach him to swim; if you can't change their attitude, you can't teach them to swim. The remediation concept leaves out attitude. When a remedial teacher is successful with a given student, as they frequently are, it is not the remedial procedure. It is because the teacher as a person has been able to change the student's attitude. Only then can he or she become successful in learning the material.

For all we know about the importance of attitude and for all the difference we know attitude makes, it seems we, as teachers, know very little about it. Consider this, "Have you ever had a course in "changing attitude?" Have you had a two-week unit in your methods course on attitude? Do you really know what attitude is? If I gave you a kid with a "bad attitude" toward math, one who says, "I hate math. It stinks!" Could you change his/her attitude? If so, how would you do it? Could you explain how you would go about it?"

A Definition of Attitude

A simplified definition; attitude is a predisposition. When someone says, "Let's go fishing." If I have had some good experiences on previous fishing trips, I might say Hooray! But, if I hate the smell of the bait and the slimly fish and get seasick in a rowboat, I might exclaim yeeeccch! We are both predisposed to fishing, and respond in a predictable consistent manner toward its mention. We both have an attitude toward it.

My own experience has been that you must first change their attitude, before you can teach them. Obviously, he or she must change his or her own attitude. Thus, the real question is, "Can you cause him or her to change his or her attitude?" If so, "How do you do it?" How often have we seen a learning problem become a behavior problem, and then work on the behavior instead of the learning? We wind up dealing with the symptom rather than the cause.

Changing Attitude

I know of only two ways to change an attitude. First, by my own attitude. Every student I have ever had has learned one thing from me, and I can absolutely guarantee it. What they have learned is me. (Actually what they have learned is I, but that sounds funny to a Tennessee boy.) They have learned what my attitude is—my attitude toward learning, toward them, toward other students, and my attitude toward the subject.

My students know me. They know whether I value the use of class time. They know whether I care about every student, or just about the "good" ones. They know whether I mean what I say. They know whether I care about real learning, or just answers on the test. They do not have to like my attitude, or agree with my attitude, but if they spend time with me, they will learn what my attitude is. They also know what their classmates' attitudes are. So, the first thing we have to do is make sure we have our own heads on straight and that our message is clear.

We have to do a "check up from the neck up." If we, the teachers, don't think our subject is important, why would the students? If we don't think every student can and will learn, why would they? If we don't believe in them, why would believe in themselves? Imagine taking a class where the instructor shows the class that he or she believes that every student will learn, will earn an A+, and will be a top student! As opposed to a teacher who says, "I don't give A's. This course is so tough, you'll be thankful to get a D."

Seeing it Differently

The second way we have of helping students to change their attitude is to help them see it differently. If they saw it differently, they would behave differently. If they see what I see or know what I know, they would do what I do. If a student saw that a particular unit of learning was going to affect his or her life this year, next year, and throughout his schooling, he or she would keep me after school and make me teach him or her.

There are many, many ways to get kids to see learning differently. A typical way to get them to see it differently is to break it into its parts so that they can see, "If I learn this, I could then learn that," or to feel success and want to go on. Some ways that can work well in remedial settings are role reversal, or a prestige position. An example would be making the class trouble-maker a teaching assistant, or having poor students in the junior high "tutor" kids in the primary. A good way to keep a kid from making trouble in the halls is to make him or her a hall monitor who wears a safety patrol belt and badge.

In an old book, *Developing Attitude Toward Learning,* Robert Mager says there are three sources of influence on subject matter: the conditions that surround a subject; the consequences of coming into contact with the subject; and the way others react toward a subject (modeling). He further states that people often verbalize a conviction that they cannot learn particular subject matter, and that, "Once such a behavior pattern develops, it is unlikely that it will be reversed... no teaching goal can be reached unless the student is influenced to become different in some way than he was before the instruction was undertaken."

Developmental not Remedial

The remedial concept has no place in the classroom. It is the developmental concept that needs to be used. If a kid is in first grade and doesn't know her multiplication tables, there is no problem or no concern. She is not supposed to know that. If she is in the seventh grade and doesn't know her multiplication tables, we think she needs remediation. She doesn't, she needs to learn her times tables. Slow learning is no more than coming to a task without the necessary prerequisite knowledge to do that task. What she needs is to be taught the necessary knowledge. The problem is that she is over age. She probably has a negative predisposition from already having been "presented" with the knowledge many times over. This is why it becomes an attitude problem with the kid and/or with the teacher.

Benjamin Bloom, in a book called *Human Characteristics and School Learning*, explains in a mastery learning model, that a learner comes to a given school task with two things—prior knowledge and prior attitude. As he deals with the task, he comes out with two things—new knowledge of the task and a new attitude. Unfortunately, if he does not have success with the task, the new knowledge might be "I can't do it." And the new attitude might be, "I hate this stuff."

Unless we deal with his prior attitude before repeating tasks and unless we are aware of the attitude that can develop with lack of success in the task, we are not likely to be successful in repeating the task. The farther along the kid is in school, the more generalized the attitude becomes. "I hate fractions" becomes "I hate math." and then becomes "I hate school." The more generalized the attitude becomes, the more difficult it is to deal with that attitude.

Difficult, Maybe Impossible

It is difficult to deal with the various attitudes of our "good" students. It is more difficult to deal with the attitude of our poorer performing students. It is still more difficult to deal with the attitude of students who have a history of failure. To continue to deal with them as remedial or failing students makes it virtually impossible to deal with their attitudes or to help them learn anything but more failure and hate. Combine this with teachers who don't understand the importance of teaching attitude; others who don't feel the need to change students' attitudes; and still others who don't know how to go about changing attitude even if they wanted to and remediation becomes impossible for many teachers and far too many students.

Remediation doesn't work! Changing attitudes does work; but we need to learn how!

Teacher Characteristics for Student Achievement

In our own schooling, all of us are sure to remember the good teachers we had. As we recall these teachers, we probably find that they were not all alike or even similar to each other. Each was a unique person, an individual with a variety of unique characteristics and his/her own special style, techniques, values, and methods. Knowledge of the subject was never a defining issue. My own recollections and thoughts about my good teachers are these:

Good teachers are first a people; and it is their unique human characteristics that make them memorable or outstanding teachers. I doubt that one could take a "dull person" and make him an exciting teacher. Second, because teaching involves interaction and communication, it is good interpersonal skills, abilities, and sensitivity that set them apart.

In examining my own experience as both a student and a teacher, I concluded that it is not what or how much a person knows that makes her a good teacher. If that were the case, anyone who can do math can teach math; anyone who can drive can teach driving (the way she drives, of course); and, anyone who knows how to read could teach reading. I know people who know a lot but are not good at teaching what they know.

It is not what people do that makes them good teachers. Two people can do the same thing or use the same techniques with a wide variance in success. It is what a person is. That is, it is their self-image, an authenticity as opposed to phoniness—the integrity of one's authentic self.

Various authors (Carl Rogers, Abe Maslow, and Arthur Combs) indicate the need for certain personal qualities that make a difference in the teaching-learning relationship. Specifically, they note empathy, warmth, and genuineness. Teachers with a high level of these qualities create conditions conductive to learning. Research shows differences in achievement for students with such teachers.

Empathy, Warmth, Genuineness

1. Empathy is the ability to put oneself in the student's position, to understand their inner thoughts and feelings. It is "tuning in" to the verbal and non-verbal feelings of the student. Empathy ranges in teacher attentiveness at these levels: a) Tuning out; b) Tuning in to words; c) tuning in to words and obvious feelings; d) tuning in to basic emotions and feelings.
2. Warmth is making oneself "approachable." It is listening with interest and positive regard or caring for the student. It requires unconditional acceptance with a non-evaluative demeanor. The

opposite would be lack of concern, and ranges at levels such as these: a) offering advice, approving or disapproving; b) positive caring, teacher feels responsible for the student; c) teacher communicates deep feeling and interest in a nonjudgmental manner.

3.   Genuineness is the ability of teachers to be themselves, non-defensive, and authentic. Genuine teachers lack a facade or a contrived or "rehearsed" quality. The levels of response range from a defensiveness or mechanicalness to a deep involvement with honest attention and interaction.

How do these characteristics fit with your "good" teachers? I find that my good teachers really cared about me, I thought of all of them as human as opposed to "professional." They were all real people with authentic responses and concerns. They were the ones I got to know as humans.

Each of us as teachers is unique. We do not need to "copy" others or look for "gimmicks." We need to adapt ideas and procedures that fit our own personalities and teaching styles. We need to develop our own strengths and special way of showing how much we care about our subject, our class and each of our students.

It is our interpersonal relation skills, and our willingness to expose our feelings and emotions that is the essence of the teacher-student relationship. It is going from attentiveness to active listening and then going beyond that, to genuine attention and caring and an honest desire to understand from the students perspective. We listen to the total message being communicated because we really care and want to fully understand what is behind the words. Probably, most of us know and appreciate the feeling we get when someone shows honest interest and concern for our feelings and for us.

Because we understand students' feelings and they are so much a part of our lives, we teachers sometimes forget or forego our responsibility in the teacher-student relationship. It is one thing to know a kid is hurting, it is another to show him we know; it is still another thing to make a positive action, and then to follow through with continued regard. This level of regard is what most teachers mean when they say they love kids.

Do a little self-reflection. Do you emphasize with the student in your class who is your biggest problem? Do you think the "bottom student in your class would say you are warm and approachable? Do you convey honest, genuine feelings to the kid that causes you the most problems? Thinking back to your own schooling and your own teachers, how do these three characteristics fit with the teachers you liked or disliked? Was any teacher you disliked one who "taught you well?" Do you feel you could improve these characteristics in yourself? What might you do? Where would you begin?

Think of a particular student. Is it likely that a sincere discussion with him/her might enable you to express and show one or more characteristics more clearly? If that student felt your sincerity, might it have made a difference in your relationship? Might it have changed your response to his/her behavior?

Student Self-Concept and Achievement

If we rank ordered a class of 100 students, How far down the list from the top student would we go before running out of a good self-concept? Would the thirty-sixth student think s/he is smart? Would the fiftieth student feel confident and competent? How about the seventieth? Do our teaching procedures show a positive regard for self-concept?

How Important is Self-Concept?

Without exception, every school mission statement I have seen contains a specific item dealing with student self-concept as a crucial dimension of school success. Yet most (all I have ever been associated with) schools deliberately and systematically diminish the self-concept of a significant number of students and knowingly lessen the self-concept of many others.

Many students are told every day in many ways they are inadequate. By judging students' worth and ability in relation to one another, schools communicate a message of deficiency, and incompetence. The deleterious judgments can be so subtle the injury is undetected to so cruel and brutal as to be inhumane.

Comparative Judgment

In virtually every subject, every period, every day, every student will be judged, measured, or compared by teachers, peers, and herself, either directly or by inference. As homework is collected or returned; as assignments are checked, as questions are asked, answered and discussed; as students are called on; and a tests are reviewed, administered, graded and returned, students are judged and compared.

These unfortunate comparisons, however inadvertent and self-administered, are likely to be interpreted as an assessment of the student's personal value or worth as an individual. Because the judgments are always relative, the student knows where she ranks and whether she is doing better or worse than others. She will know from grades, marks, tests, papers, parents, teachers, friends, peers, looks, remarks, jokes, comparisons, and self-assessment.

The Rich Get Rich …

Because virtually all school learning is done in groups, and most assignments and tests are the same for all, and competition is used as a basic motivational technique; constant judgment is an integral part of every class throughout the school day. And because the grading system is so omnipresent, entrenched, and emotion-ridden, it is always a topic of anxiety, discussion, and concern. In addition, because the skills necessary for success in school are similar, regardless of the subject, and because course content is sequential and interrelated, students' relative position rarely moves up or down significantly. The rich stay rich and the poor stay poor.

Lack of Learning is Cumulative

Lack of learning is cumulative. If a student gets a month behind in a subject, it doesn't mean he will stay a month behind. On the contrary, because he is a month behind, he could be expected to drop much further behind as the school year progresses. Students who are significantly behind their peers early in their schooling are especially susceptible to discouragement and demoralization.

As devastating as evaluations are, they could probably be overcome, balanced, or at least rationalized with an "I don't care" or "that's stupid stuff" attitude. But once report cards make the inadequacy public and permanent, once tracking and grouping make the ranking official, and once the social stratification is clearly established, the low ranking is likely to become more marked. Neither public denial nor self-denial will have any effect.

Negative Attitude

Continued failure, marginal failure, and relative failure, even acceptable grades perceived as unacceptable or undeserved, often produce a negative attitude toward school, teachers, and specific subjects in most cases. Over a period of time, the negative attitude directed at school can easily be directed inwardly to a negative view of self. After years of defending her ego against the barrage of negative judgments and accumulation of negative self-concept, denial is no longer an option.

Then comes the added insult. Because she is having trouble in school, she is probably having trouble at home. Hating school, disliking subjects and school personnel, failing tests, skipping school, ignoring assignments and homework, students lose the motivation even to try or to act interested. Failure to put forth effort, a defeatist attitude, and the resulting embarrassment make getting along with parents difficult.

A Double Whammy

The trouble at school and the trouble at home make a double whammy on her life. Home and school are a student's life. Few could survive the twin assault without permanent scars. And unless she can find some refuge in the nonacademic areas of school or personal life or outside of the home and school life, she is likely to seek self-esteem through the only route always open to her. Students are never powerless; they are simply forced to find power through marginally acceptable or illicit means such as comrades-in-arms, gangs, drugs, alcohol, and other forms of peer-pressure activities. "If you tell me I'm no good, I'll show you I am good—but not on your terms or turf. I'll show you I can get drunker, get more money (by whatever means) and gain more attention (however negatively) than you ever imagined."

Predictable

I'm not sure how some students are able to escape the predictable downfall caused by chronic failure, although certainly there are those who survive the double whammy. If students can gain recognition through athletics; if they have a sociable personality or good interpersonal skills; if they can get by on looks, social savvy, or marketable work skills, and if they have some friendly adult connections, they might at least have a chance to overcome the predictable slide down the slippery slope. These exceptions notwithstanding, alienation is predestined. If schools set out deliberately to marginalize students, driving them to rebellious sub-cultures, they would do precisely what they are doing with those students most at risk.

A Starting Point

With these concerns in mind, here is a suggested starting point for identifying some of the problems and the dimensions of the problems of failure, low self-concept, grading, and schooling as it is too frequently done.

First, there are the timeless, perennial, traditional problems about which every educator complains and about which nothing is ever done, including

- Initial school entrance based on chronological age
- Lock-step, grade level movement each year
- Lack of viable alternatives to social promotion or failure
- Students all on the same time schedule
- Biases and prejudices, both deliberate and unintentional
- Irrelevant, obsolete curriculum
- Comparative, frequent and public assessments
- Bureaucratic, top-down education demands and control
- Lack of teacher autonomy to respond individually

Second, if schooling is mandatory, learning must be appropriate. If a student can't learn the required curriculum, the curriculum must be changed. If they can learn, but do not, it is the schooling process that is a failure, not the student. Students are required to present themselves; after that they are the responsibility of the system and its policies. To compel them to come and then flunk them is inhumane, insane, and unnecessary.

Third, if self-concept is truly important to learning success and if all kids are required to attend, then norm standards, competition, grading, honor rolls, and failure have no place in school. So long as there is a comparison ranking of students, there will be guaranteed, built-in failure. Even if every student made the honor roll there would be ranking from top to bottom of the honor roll, and probably a noting of who got there first or with the most ease.

For Every Winner there is a Loser

"Winners" will always be at the expense of "losers." There cannot be good students unless there are also bad students; otherwise, they would just be students. Schools cannot have a valedictorian without the class goat, nor the upper third of the graduating class without the bottom third, or above average without below average.

Fourth, the world has been changing rapidly while schools have remained virtually unchanged. New technology is here, but textbooks, worksheets, and rote memorization with its drill and kill is still the norm. Family structures and values have changed, but schools complain about families instead of adjusting to the changes. Society, the world, and the economy base have changed and are continuing to change while schools struggle to understand, but fail to act.

Fifth, for all the restructuring and reform; for all the concern for diversity, equity, equality, ethnicity and cultural diversity; for all the rhetoric on differentiation, constructivism; and for all the involvement of federal and state politicians with mandates and achievement-by-test-intimidation, the most fundamental learning concepts are still ignored. For example we know that students do not learn by:

- Sitting passively in rows having their ears talked at.
- Learning the same lesson at the same time.
- Reading sterile textbooks and answering inane questions.
- Identifying with a teacher they don't like or want to be like.
- Studying content in which they see no sense.
- Memorizing irrelevant, fragmented meaningless material.
- Working under pressure from threat, anxiety, and coercion.
- Learning a little bit of each subject, each period, each day.

Three Important Concepts

What needs to be done? There are three concepts that can make the most difference and toward which schools might move to insure success for every student:

1. The basic student-teacher relationship should be built on mutual trust, democratic interaction, and mutual respect in the classroom and school.
2. Learning communities at all levels, should be built on a positive attitude, cooperation, esprit de corps, high morale, and high expectations.

3. Increased student responsibility is possible only through increased student participation, and involvement in decisions affecting their learning.

Change the Foundation, Not the Floor Plan

Those responsible for all the mandatory testing laws have suceeded in rearranging the floor plan rather than restructuring the foundation. A good self-concept and the mandated increase in student achievement, closing the gap, reduction of drop-outs, at-risk problems, and failures is not possible for many students without changing the grading policies and the many known elements that predestines failure.

Schools must first determine what they want the students to value, desire, and appreciate. Schools must ask the question, "What do we want students to be like; what do we want them to understand, to become?" Then schools must determine what needs to be done to achieve those goals. If they want every student to succeed, to achieve, and to become productive, self-activated, and independent, they must offer the experiences that will guide them and teach them.

A Remarkably Successful Program
For At-Risk Students

There are textbooks, workbooks, manuals, manipulative devices, and gadgets of all sorts designed to remediate communication disorders. While the publishers claim many of these to be appropriate for junior high school, the fact is that there is a complete and utter void of remedial material appropriate for junior high school or secondary school. However, from my perspective, I am not so much concerned with the absence of remedial material as I am with the absence of a satisfactory rationale under which remedial techniques may be applied.

I Am A Classroom Teacher

My perspective is that of a classroom teacher. I am not a researcher, or a remediation specialist, or a learning disabilities teacher—I am a teacher of "kids who have trouble in school," or "kids they kick out of other classes" and my concern is the here and now.

I am glad that there are people working on theory, etiology, and hypothetical constructs. I am concerned for the particular kids in a particular classroom—mine! My concern is for their beliefs, feelings, attitudes, and ideas. My concern is for what to do tomorrow morning at 8:30 when my kids show up with a need to be taught.

Because my concern is for the attitude and self-concept of the kids as a prerequisite to improving achievement, what is done is not nearly as important as how and why it is done. Specifically, the child must understand, in terms that are meaningful to him, what is needed and why it is needed. And, I must know how he sees it and how he feels about it.

A Tutoring Program

The remedial procedure I have found most beneficial for students with a history of failure and a negative attitude is a tutoring program in which the disabled learner becomes the tutor rather than the tutored. Motivationally, this situation is ideal. The role reversal gives the tutor some genuine prestige and enables him to see the learner from a different perspective. One seventh-grade boy came back from a tutoring assignment with a first-grader and said, "Mr. Page, I was supposed to teach him number facts but he keeps running off down the hall and I have to chase after him." I didn't have to say, "Yes, it is hard to teach someone who doesn't want to learn isn't it?" He saw it, felt it, was embarrassed by it.

Tutoring is obviously a good way to get an older student to work at a lower grade level without the usual stigma associated with remediation. He can work at as low a grade level as he chooses, or, as will be beneficial to him. Just recently I observed a seventh-grade boy, who was two years over age, carrying around a third-grade math workbook, deliberately exposing it so that other seventh graders would say, "What are you doing with a third-grade math book?" and he would reply proudly, "Oh, I teach it!"

Tutoring helps to show the tutor that learning is a process. By analyzing lower level tasks, a sort of "task analysis," the tutor begins to see that learning is more than just a matter of luck, it is a matter of determining appropriate steps and then being committed to going through those steps, getting help when needed.

To profit from the tutoring, the child does not necessarily have to work in his area of weakness or at the specific level of his deficiency. A project in New York City showed that some high school students, who were potential dropouts, were paid to go into ghettos to teach kindergarten and first grade children reading readiness skills. In seven months of tutoring the average gain in reading levels for the tutors was three and a half years on the average. Perhaps the self-esteem involved in being appreciated, and seeing themselves as worthwhile, and becoming interested in somebody and some thing, along with the prestige, practice and interest accounted for the difference.

A Wide Range of Involvement

A typical reaction to the tutoring program is, "How can you have this kind of kid tutoring kids in the lower grades who are so vulnerable?" The tutoring involvement can range from a behind-the-scene activity, to helping a first grader learn to tie his shoes—to actually teaching basic concepts. In some cases we start with a "methods course" in preparation for tutoring. We have discussion sessions on the value of good manners and appearance, and teach them how to prepare lesson plans. As we use it, each child develops his own methods ideas according to what he wants to teach and how he plans to go about it.

A second phase of the tutoring is materials preparation. The children create worksheets according to what they plan to teach. They do everything from making pictures to go with consonant sounds, to making puzzles or maps of the United States, or creating lists of words with the long vowel sounds. In some cases we have even had a second grade teacher come before the class to request our class, as a group, to make certain materials for her. We use a lot of first and second grade activity books in our room for ideas.

A Wide Variety of Jobs

We encourage those kids who are interested, to develop plays and skits, and presentations of various sorts, to be presented to first or second grade classes. Sometimes they make up rather elaborate plays and write their own songs (parodies).

Some of the kids, who are motorically capable, make over-sized thermometers, or giant rulers and charts, or mechanical objects, as classroom aids. One eighth grade boy got a lot of satisfaction from simply sanding and varnishing the kindergartner's wooden blocks, after he found out kids were getting splinters from playing with them.

From the standpoint of actual tutoring, one of the best-liked activities is helping kindergartners learn to catch a ball or walk a balance beam. A phase of the tutoring program popular with some of the junior high tutors is working with the elementary coach. There are many fairly passive types of tutoring involvement, such as, listening to kids read, holding up flash cards, assisting the teacher or supervising games or spotting on the trampoline.

Active tutoring may include anything from giving make-up tests to teaching mathematics concepts or mentoring and coaching a variety of activities. Sometimes they simply sit next to their student to keep him/her on task.

A School Bus Widened Our Range

The program has been in use for four years in the University City School District, in St. Louis County where a school bus is now used to deliver some 40 junior high children to five different elementary schools on an hourly basis during the school day. Our school pays the bus driver's hourly wage; the district pays the bus cost and the employee benefits.

As the elementary teachers saw their students improve, the request for tutors far exceeded the number of students in our program, so we included other junior high slow learners in the supply of tutors provided. The value to the children being taught in the elementary schools is every bit as impressive as the value to the tutor.

Making their Own Materials

An especially practical remedial procedure is that of having the children make their own materials. This procedure reduces the need to find commercially prepared material; gets the kids involved in the activity, utilizes more of his modes; and is great for building self-esteem. The things that we have found most useful in this procedure are: (1) raw materials including such things as assorted arts and crafts supplies, boxes, cardboard, and sheets of flannel material, (2) machines and equipment including a copy machine, a paper cutter, lighted tracing box, and assorted tools, (3) samples, ideas, and suggestions that can inspire the creating of materials, and (4) trips to a school supply store and game stores.

Here are some materials and ideas that we have used:

- Use plain one-inch wooden counting cubes as dice. Kids can put anything from Roman numerals to phonic blends. They can put the part they're having trouble with in a different color magic marker and can devise rules for playing the dice game according to what they need most to practice.

- Instead of having an entire set of phonics wheels, have just one or two as samples so the kid can make his own phonics wheels appropriate to the sounds with which he is having the most trouble. My kids make a lot of "blank" materials.
- Catalogs of school supplies give kids all kinds of suggestions of things they can make to help themselves learn or tutor. They "scrounge" raw materials from many sources.
- Activity books that show puzzles, mazes, and games can be traced by the pupil or adapted and copied. They can also be pasted over and reused.
- Children can make flannel boards and design and cut out their own flannel characters.
- Some children make manipulative devices such as counting frames, geo boards, place value devices, and games of all kinds.
- They can adapt games such as scrabble or anagrams by changing the rules according to what they most need to practice.
- Projects and joint efforts of all kinds can be made. Children can make things for each other and can try out their materials on others.

Materials Upgraded from Elementary to Junior High

- One valuable aspect of the kids making their own materials is that of upgrading or adapting materials, which were originally designed for lower grades, to the junior high level.
- We introduced the Peabody Kit as being good but too babyish. The kids promptly began making their own by replacing pictures that were more appropriate and by writing their own activities.

One excellent project was a group effort in making an SRA type kit on "newspaper reading." They would paste newspaper articles on cards, make out the comprehension questions and answer cards and even design and decorate the box. They wound up with sections of news stories, feature stories, editorials, cartoons, comic strips, columns, and even want ads. Once the kit was complete nearly everyone in class went entirely through it.

Clipping ads out of newspapers and making word problems based on the advertised items made math workbooks. Some of the sections of the workbook included money problems, two-step problems and a full range of fraction problems. The making of the materials was as valuable as using the materials, and made them more meaningful.

The potential for this program is virtually unlimited. Besides the self-concept factor, the two aspects of the program that I consider most valuable are that the kids become involved in active and creative and cooperative roles and that the teacher is required to explain the purpose of the activity so that the child can know what he is to come up with, and what adaptations he will need. Or quite simply, "The best way to learn something is to teach it!"

The following article is a published transcript of a presentation given by Bill Page in 1968. It is an idea whose time is still here after 37 years. The article is provided here to show how little things in education really change. Cross-grade tutoring has been around and has been used since the days of the one-room country school. It has also been around in articles published in the last few years in major education journals.

A Junior High Remedial Program
A TUTORING PROGRAM WITH UNBELIEVABLE RESULTS
Published by
SELECTED PAPERS ON LEARNING
From A Presentation By Bill Page Given at the
7th Annual International Conference of the Association for Children
with Learning Disabilities In Philadelphia, PA
1968

Now 37 years old, the article was run to show how little things in education really change. Cross-grade tutoring has been around and has been used since the days of the one room country school. It has also been around in articles published in the last few years in major education journals.

Below is the article that "started "our tutoring program going.

Article from St. Louis Post-Dispatch--Sept. 17, 1966

TUTORING PROGRAM FOR CHILDREN IMPROVES YOUNG TEACHERS TOO

NEW YORK, Sept. 17 (UPI) -- A one-way project aimed at helping scholastically retarded Black and Puerto Rican children in New York's lower East Side schools has surprised its sponsors by becoming a two-way improvement program. The teachers, youngsters themselves, get smarter too.

This was reported today by Robert D. Cloward, research associate at Columbia University's School of Social Research. The school evaluates research programs of the Mobilization for Youth, which created the New York project, known as the Homework Helpers Program.

Since the program began in 1963 more than 600 high school students have worked as tutors with about 2000 children in 16 lower East Side elementary schools.

Cloward said that reading levels of all participants were significantly improved but the big surprise was that the abilities of the high school tutors--many of them poor students themselves at the start- - "surged ahead three-and-one-half years on the average in a period of seven months."

As a result, Cloward said, an effort will be made to enlist as tutors more and girls who are doing borderline school work High school dropouts also be encouraged to join the project as tutors. The belief is that many might then be inspired to resume schooling.

The young tutors are paid for their work. With the cooperation of the city's Board of Education, 150 high school students will be hired this school year and be paid $12.00 a week for eight hours of tutoring.

Murphy, the Tutor

Reversing their roles and making problem learners the tutors, made the difference, not just academically but in many other ways.

A nineteen-year-old senior high school boy, with the first name Murphy, had no credits in high school and was reading at a low elementary grade level. Murphy had recently transferred into our suburban high school from a special education program in urban St Louis. As a small suburb district we had only a remedial type program at the senior high, with nothing to offer him. The counselor at his high school called to ask if I could take him in my junior high school program for "kids who have trouble in school." After six weeks of trying, they had given up on Murphy.

A Program For Low Achievers

The program at Hanley Junior High was a funded research project called Project Enable. The project used a tutoring program in which seventh graders, whose skills were too low for the regular junior high program, became tutors of primary level students as a means of improving the self concept of the tutor and giving him/her reason or excuse to study and read at any elementary or primary level. The seventh-graders collected books and built a room library of pre-primer books, which they read into tape recorders and to each other as a way of practicing reading and improving expression. Their goal was getting the opportunity to go to the nearby elementary school to read to primary students.

The Problem Kids Became Tutors

I was afraid of the stigma of Murphy's being in the junior high, although he was a small slightly built kid who was shy and quiet and might have passed as a junior high student. So I agreed to let him stop by the junior high school for two hours every morning on his way to high school, to ride the bus with my kids who tutored at three elementary schools daily for a two-hour session. To introduce him to the program, I suggested that he observe for a few days, to see if he might like to tutor some first graders.

Murphy really wasn't prepared to tutor at all, so he sat on a bench in the cafetorium watching several tutoring sessions from a distance. The second day, a fourth grader chose to sit by him while waiting to go back to class. When the young boy asked Murphy for the time, Murphy pointed to the clock and subsequently found out the kid could not tell time. Telling time was one thing Murphy was able to do, so with help, he set about teaching the fourth grader, using paper plates with moveable hands attached, ditto sheets, and an old alarm clock with no glass cover.

A Time-Telling Clinic

In a short time, not only had the fourth grader learned, Murphy had a "time-telling clinic" going. He would teach a child to tell time, and the teacher would send him another kid to start the process over again. Murphy worked himself out of a job by teaching time telling to some two dozen kids in three weeks. The principal of the elementary school said another school requested Murphy's tutoring service.

Another boy in the program named Mike, set up a shoe-tying clinic using a similar model and making special practice props for lacing and holding knot loops. By tying a black and white shoestring together and using the black part for the left hand and white for the right hand, the learner, using a shoebox with lacing holes, graduating to a boot and to his own shoe held in his hands, learned to tie the knot, and tie his shoes.

What Have You Done To Murphy

Barely a month from the time Murphy began tutoring, I got a call from the high school counselor saying, Murphy's teachers want to know what you have done to him. He has changed so dramatically that the teachers can't understand it and would like to meet with you and Kay, the other program teacher, to learn about what has happened to Murphy.

At the meeting, we learned that Murphy had been known to smile only twice in the six-week period the high school teachers had had him. He kept his chin on his chest and would not acknowledge the teachers when he passed them in the hall, he had never made a response in class, voluntarily or otherwise, and he had never turned in a single homework paper or class paper, no matter how simple.

The High School Tries Tutoring

Now the two remedial teachers reported that, in the past two weeks he had been smiling almost continuously, he greeted them in the halls, he had volunteered answers in class, and he had turned in assignments every day for the past week. The two high school teachers subsequently set up the opportunity for their classes to tutor in an elementary school across the street from the high school. Murphy, as an experienced tutor, actually became a resource, helping them in setting up the program.

Self-Concept Makes the Difference

While no research was done on Murphy's transformation, we know there was a transformation. I personally attribute the changes to the increase in confidence and the self-image improvement wrought by elementary age students showing genuine, unrestrained appreciation for him.

Kids Need Encouragement

Unfortunately, schools usually emphasize negativity in grades, trust, responsibility, fears, threats, and intimidation as an integral part of daily routine. To build and improve self-concept emphasis needs to be on encouragement and positive regard in trust, responsibility with reduction in fears, threats, and intimidation.

The lowest level kids, from the time they start in school, see them selves as poor learners, non-readers and perceive themselves as lacking ability. Lack of learning accumulates, and kids are forced to give up. We know what is wrong, what to do and where to start. What more do we need to begin making a difference in the lives of problem learners?

Labels Are For Jelly Jars

On our farm, we stored our canned goods in the dark, damp cellar. Even in the daylight it was impossible to tell raspberry jelly from blackberry or grape without labels. Labels have many important uses—but not for kids.

"I have never done anything to, for, or with a kid because s/he was "mentally retarded." As a teacher, I do things because the kid is a human being who has ways of responding to me in my role and to the context in which we interact. If his/her manner of responding is a problem to me, or needs improving, I make changes in me and or in the context. The kid may then, in turn, be more likely to change him/herself."

The value of any educational diagnosis is that it can lead to understanding, change, correction, prevention, or remediation. To diagnose just for the sake of diagnosis or to diagnose using a jumble of meaningless jargon is a vice that neither kids nor teachers can afford.

If the diagnosis is, she's immature; the remediation would be to make her more mature. If the diagnosis is a low IQ, the remediation would be to raise his IQ. If problem is premature birth.......well, er...we need to determine what, if anything is wrong and deal with the manifestations. Specialized professionals need to take responsibility for research, etiology, or preventive measures. I, the teacher, deal with the kid and her problem, as it exists, regardless of the causes, or reasons for the problems.

The crucial questions in diagnoses are these: "Does this diagnosis lead to decisions within your realm of responsibility? Does the diagnosis place blame on the kid, his parents, or excuse the teacher from doing her job? Does the diagnosis lead to remediation of the diagnosed problems? What is the purpose of the diagnosis? For whom is the diagnosis? Labels can be useful in communication but are frequently of little or no value in remediation.

Labels Have a Place; But Not In Remediation

"Appendicitis" is a useful term for helping parents understand a child's illness. It is also appropriate to use this term explaining his absence to the school and his hospital stay to his grandmother. But to do something about the appendicitis condition requires specific procedures, knowledge, skills, plans, medical expertise, and complex decisions. The term appendicitis is an effective way to communicate about a problem, but the label is not important to those who must make decisions and take action to remedy the problem.

Educational labels and diagnostic terms can be useful in talking about a kid's difficulties. Expressions such as, "He is culturally deprived. He can't remember from one day to the next. She is above average. She has ADHD. Or, she is immature." can be used for reporting statistics such as: "In our school, 16 percent of our kids are learning disabled." Or for record keeping purposes: "She is two grade levels below average in reading." Labels may also be useful to those specialists concerned with etiology and prevention of problems. Labels are convenient and often adequate in communicating between professional about a kid, but they are of no use whatsoever to anyone trying to help a kid learn, improve, achieve, or change his/her behavior.

A Description In Lieu of a Label

Diagnosing a kid as "retarded," "hyperactive," or "ADHD" can be useful to anyone who has a need to discuss the kid, compile data, transmit information, or screen for grouping or budgeting. But if I want to change or improve a kid's behavior, the label is useless and may even be detrimental. In lieu of a label, however accurately applied, what I need is an accurate, complete, detailed description of his behavior, in relation to me, my concerns, my specific teaching content, my responsibility, and accompanying conditions and context stated in language that is meaningful to me personally and to my teaching circumstances and goals.

I need to know how he responds to the specific material I teach and to the accompanying techniques and conditions. She can't remember must be followed by, this spelling word, these spelling words I assign, the way I assign them, the strategies I use in relation to the learning conditions, timing, and other circumstances and contexts.

To say "I am fat" is a label: to say, "I eat too much" is a description. To say, "I eat too much between meals" is more descriptive. To say, "I eat too much ice cream between meals and before bedtime" is still more descriptive and could be further described in terms of fat content, quantity, caloric, and nutritional factors. A detailed analysis such as this has an obvious remediation objective.

Label versus Description

The first step to a meaningful, useful diagnosis is distinguishing between a label and a description. Using the word "is" probably makes the phrase a label; using an action verb such as "does" very likely makes it a description:

He is "lazy" is a label. He "sleeps in class" is a description.

She is "immature" is a label. She "cries often" is a description

He is disruptive is a label. He shoves and hits kids is a description.

The second step is to refine the description and decide the conditions under which the behavior occurs. She "sleeps in class every Monday morning," or "She cries when I discuss his/her written class work." The more accurate, detailed and complete the description, the more useful it can be in determining the remedial strategies.

The third step is to get the kid's input, find out how the kid sees it. I need to know whether she sees it as a problem. I need to know what her attitude is toward changing the behavior. I need to know her reasons for working on the problem and his level of concern. If the kid sees no problem with the behavior, sees its solution as hopeless, doesn't want to change or doesn't trust me to help; it would require a very different starting point. This is crucial in one-on-one tutoring. There is no need to tutor the kid if she doesn't acknowledge the problem and request help.

The fourth step is to ask myself, "So what?" What is my real concern about the behavior? If a kid habitually comes to class late, my way of dealing with his lateness would be quite different if the problem were the work he misses, his responsibility for following rules, the disruption to classmates, the principal's interest about my class control, the example to other students. or my curiosity about what he is doing while not in class. I must decide the specific problem to deal with it.

An Example

A colleague, Marie Alexander, who teaches third grade was telling me about one of her students. She said quite simply, "Tony is clumsy." That, of course, is a label, so I asked her to give me some details. With my help, we went through the four steps of the diagnostic process.

1. The description: "He stumbles over his own feet." "He trips when there is nothing to trip on."
2. A specific description: "He frequently bumps into kid's desks just walking up the aisle." "He hits one foot into the other anytime he walks more than a few steps."
3. The kid's input: Tony says, "I don't want to do it. I just can't help falling or hitting into desks. I don't like the kids laughing at me, either."
4. So What: What is the teacher's specific problem with Tony's stumbling? Marie said, "I am concerned that he bumps into the desks disturbing not only the kid in the seat but creating a general disturbance and distracting the entire class." We included the embarrassment of Tony being laughed at in our consideration.

NOTE: The approach to the resolution of the problem would have been an entirely different matter if Marie had expressed a concern for potential physical injury, coordination problems for the "clumsiness" being considered symptomatic of other problems, or for its interference with her lessons, her liability, or her responsibility to the parents.

The Solution

This diagnostic process led to these considerations:

1. Move Tony to a front row seat so he doesn't have to walk up the aisle. Widen the aisle or put him in the row next to the wall with the chalkboard ledge to hang on to.
2. Go to him instead of having him come up the aisle. Let him be the last one out as the class leaves the room.
3. Place "little dot marks" or tape on the floor to assist him with foot placement.
4. Mix the desks or rearrange the room so there is no aisle.
5. Have a friend "guide" him or get things for him.
6. There might be many other considerations including proper shoe fit, restrictive clothing, habit, or even brain damage. Perhaps removing his shoes might make him more aware of his foot placement.

A discussion with Tony led to the mutually determined decision that he would "be more careful" and he would "try harder"—his words. We accepted this as a start, a trial, and we added the dimension of slowing down and taking more deliberate steps. If "being careful" didn't work, Ms. Alexander's next choice would be to move him to a front seat even though he was fairly tall. She also discussed ways she and Tony could get his classmates to help, especially in accepting his effort to improve and refraining from laughing. It worked!

In this instance, the solution worked because the effort was at a more conscious level, and the reduced frequency of the bumping with the lessening of the impact on those occasions when he did stumble, reduced the problem significantly. Had it not worked, there were other approaches available. For instance, on trips up the aisle to get materials, a friend could have gone for him; as the class went to phys ed, he could have gone last; the teacher could have put small marks on the floor to help him place his feet more carefully; or he might have taken off his shoes to make him more conscious of the placement of his feet.

Labels can be convenient for communicating about a problem; but to make decisions about its solution, we must first note the specific circumstances involved.

Our ability to adequately describe the particular situation and its unique conditions are necessary for an appropriate solution. Too often, the fourth step, "So What?" of the procedure listed above is omitted or taken for granted. Even worse, teachers sometimes feel they have to deal with all of the possible solutions rather than to narrow it to a specific, manageable problem.

The Teacher Is The Difference

There are many factors that can make a difference in student achievement, but:

THE TEACHER <u>IS</u> THE DIFFERENCE

Textbooks don't teach kids,

Administrators don't teach kids

Rules don't teach kids

Tests don't teach kids

Block schedules don't teach kids

State departments of education don't teach kids

Support staffs don't teach kids

Politicians don't teach kids.

Teachers teach kids!

TEACHERS DON'T GET TO CHOOSE:

Their working conditions, rooms, or materials;

Their students or their parents;

Their administrators or their colleagues;

Their class loads, schedules or student-teacher ratio,

Their period or school day length.

TEACHERS DON'T <u>MAKE</u> A DIFFERENCE; THEY <u>ARE</u> THE DIFFERENCE IN KIDS LEARNING

Kids don't know or care much about school reform, high stakes testing, inclusion, site-based management or assessment-driven curriculum – they just come to school. They have good days and bad days, Some days they learn a lot; some days seem to be a waste of time. Whether they learn a little of a lot depends on what their teacher decides to do or not to do.

TEACHERS TEACH KIDS—THEY DO IT BY:

Their minute-to-minute decisions; their communication skills and their knowledge.

They can provide motivation; they can make a kid feel competent and confident.

They can provide interest and offer opportunity; they can facilitate a kid's learning.

They make a difference in the kids attitude, participation and in his/her life.

THE TEACHER <u>IS</u> THE DIFFERENCE IN KIDS' LEARNING

Kids Are Never Not Learning

Only nine percent of a kid's life is spent in school, but they are never <u>not</u> learning.

Don't worry about what kids are learning; worry about what they are doing. Don't worry that kids aren't listening to you; worry that they are observing you.

The current catch phrase, "Every child Can learn!" is misleading. It should say, "Every child Does learn." Learning is a natural, effortless, continuous, ongoing phenomenon occupying every waking moment, every day in the life of every human being from before s/he is born until s/he dies and perhaps beyond. Kids learn what they live, what they are experiencing. And, they are living and experiencing every moment of their lives. Since their lives and experiences are so uniquely different from one another, kids come to school with enormous differences in their learning, emotions, knowledge, attitudes, interests, and abilities.

What is the School's Role?

Based solely on school's schedules and class policies, the U.S. Department of Education estimates that between birth and eighteen years of age, a student will spend only nine percent of his/her life in school. The other ninety-one percent is spent somewhere else. It is the "somewhere else" that should be our concern. For some kids the "somewhere else" takes place, in a community and culture rich with resources offering experiences that coincide with in-school learning. While for others their daily experiences are the same ones repeated over and over, and are amidst fewer resources not likely to relate to school learning goals.

Since out-of-school experiences obviously contribute to the variety of learning gaps among kids of differing background, cultural, class, and ethnic experiences, the key issue, the only real issue, is what the schools' role, accountability and mission actually are in its limited share of a kid's learning. The kid's nine percent represents a hundred percent of the schools' involvement and contribution.

School's Responsibility is to Mediate Learning

School is the one common experience every kid has. Not all kids have a home, a religion or even living parents, but every kid goes to school where there is a high degree of commonality and societal control of associations and experiences. The responsibility of schools, and therefore teachers, is to initiate, provide, and contribute to desirable experiences. More importantly, schools' responsibility is to mediate, reconcile, and enhance the differing experiences and resultant learning of each child.

Whatever his professional preparation, a teacher is first of all a person. He offers himself his own unique experiences, personality, values, emotions, and beliefs as experiences available to his students. But, recognizing the individuality of each kid and understanding the personal, unique experience base, a teacher must begin by accepting the complexity, diversity, and uniqueness of the kid's experiences, while presenting and building new experiences together. The education offered in school should be one of providing, creating, uniting, integrating, harmonizing, enhancing, and mediating each kid's experiences in relation to those that society values and for which, through education, schools declare and accept responsibility.

Following are the maxims of experiential learning likely to be occurring in any given kid's life, in any given classroom, and any given moment. This list cannot be exhaustive, nor the items distinct.

1. *Everyone in a kid's life is his/her "teacher."* Everyone with whom the kid has a relationship influences the kid precisely to the extent of the quality, involvement, or interaction in that relationship. Siblings, other family members, friends, relatives, visitors, neighbors, playmates, and classmates are teachers throughout his or her life.

2. *Everything in a kid's life experiences is his/her "teachers."* Television programs, computers, and computer games rank high among a kid's "teachers" church, nursery school, sports, home, apartment, playground, Wal-Mart, pets, community center, the mall, radio, CDs, magazines, formal and informal organizations teach kids, undesirable, misleading and erroneous information as well as enlightening information.

3. *Books, stories, video's, movies, MTV, entertainers, advertisements, and vicarious experiences are important teachers in kid's learning.* Associations with, participation in, and observation of other people's lives are a kid's constant teachers. Vicarious experiences such as witnessing another kid's reaction, seeing him/her being hurt, or watching a dramatic scene in a movie, or the nightly news can be significant learning experiences and make lasting impressions.

4. *Kids' worst classroom teacher, best classroom teacher and those in between all "taught" them—something.* Teachers have taught different lessons including erroneous lessons, but each has taught lasting, quality lessons. Kids are always learning. They

learn to be negative, positive and neutral about their ability, their learning, themselves, others, curriculum, school and "school stuff." They are constantly developing attitudes, drawing conclusions, building knowledge, and making inferences.

5. *Kids learn from the company they keep.* Early in a kid's life she usually has as "company," a family she did not choose; and grows among relatives, friends, and neighbors, but further along the way, she selects, from among available choices, those with whom she associates or identifies. As teenagers, they can develop close life-long friendships that will impact their lives. They learn to talk, walk, dress, think, perceive, and adorn themselves like their chosen friends, selected role models, and people with whom they identify.

6. *What kids learn is primarily a matter of socialization and community.* Kid's associations influence their leisure time, interests, hobbies, choices, recreation, and activities. Whether we collect cards, play cards, or send cards; even food preferences are mostly a matter of our environment, culture and many, varied sub-cultures of which we become a part.

7. *Everything kids experience is learned.* They learn to spell our confusing, complicated words incorrectly as well as correctly. Kids learn to study or learn to avoid study; they learn to do homework or learn not to do homework; kids learn bad manners, habits, and hygiene as well as good manners, habits, and hygiene. A kid walks slump shouldered because that is what s/he

learned, not because s/he failed to learn to walk with his/her shoulders pulled back.

8. *Emotions, feelings, attitudes, and senses are the triggers for learning.* Whether kids love or hate; care deeply or not at all; see learning as worthwhile or useless will determine his/her attention to, interest in and his/her pursuit of learning. Kids will learn in proportion to the intensity of their feelings; if they feel strongly about the subject or the teacher, they learn, if they don't care, they don't learn what is intended, whatever else they might learn.

9. *Learning is constructed as a personal, individual experience.* Learning is constructed on prior knowledge, unique perceptions, and individual experiences. We can't just transfer information into kid's heads. They must filter new facts and learning through their existing knowledge and experience to derive personal meaning and understanding from any new knowledge.

10. *If a kid is struggling and confused s/he cannot be learning (except perhaps what it is like to struggle and be confused.)* The brain can process and retain only those things that are meaningful, that make sense. It cannot receive or deal with nonsense. Struggling is a manifestation of the lack of meaning, lack of prerequisite knowledge or lack of understanding. He needs help with meaning, prerequisites, or understanding rather than harder work, more effort, pressure, or struggle.

138

11. *Coercion, anxiety, and intimidation hinder the learning process.* Threats usually activate survival behaviors and defense mechanisms but they impede the learning process. Under threat, the brain focuses on survival not on learning. We need to eliminate or at least reduce coercion to enhance and encourage learning.

12. *There is no such thing as a kid "Not paying attention."* The brain is constantly paying attention to something. In the classroom, kid's brains select from among competing stimuli whether it be from other kids, outside noises, or other environmental factors. At best, forcing a kid to pay attention usually gets him to "act" as though he is paying attention. Lack of attention to the lesson is feedback to the teacher about the lesson not the kid's inattention.

13. *The brain is constantly receiving and discarding information.* The brain is more like a sieve than a sponge, with most information passing right through. If relevant information makes a "connection" as it enters the brain, it goes into the working or short-term memory. If the information is kept only to pass a test, it will be forgotten after the test, unless it is further shifted into long-term memory. This shift requires meaningful association with existing long-term memory already in the brain. The more kids learn, the more they can and will learn.

14. *Learning and memory require understanding and comprehension.* Questioning, discussing, interacting, organizing,

explaining, applying, debating, interacting, and discovering can enhance memory. Using progressive levels of thinking such as in Bloom's Taxonomy is an ideal way to help students learn and remember. Memory requires relevance, organization, and association.

15. *Everything a kid learns is in a context that is also learned as a part of the whole.* Learning and the learning conditions cannot be separated. The context in which learning occurs is an integral part of the learning experience. A kid cannot learn something without there being circumstances in which learning takes place; nor can there be conditions of learning without something to be learned. The "why, what, when, where, who, and how," of learning are always part of the learning. The "why" of learning or reason for learning precedes the others.

16. *Language is a resource that limits or expands learning.* Lack of familiarity with the native language, limited vocabulary, restricted conversation, lack of comprehension in written language, and lack of familiarity with colloquialisms, localisms, slang, and usage significantly limits a kid's experiences. Conversely, language rich with variety, large vocabulary, varied conversations, and divergent topics can expand learning experiences. It even increases thinking and reasoning ability, not to mention social status, acceptance, and willingness to participate.

17. *The only measure of a kid's learning is his/her use or display of it.* Learning is whatever is retained from his/her lessons, teaching or experiences. While there are many ways to measure or assess learning kids have done in school; one simple way to determine key aspects of their learning is to ask them how they feel about their education—maybe an "exit poll" interview. If kids think school is irrelevant, and boring; if they think history is memorizing dates; if they don't vote, read books or newspapers; if they think they are not good at math; if they think the good parts of school were the extra curricular activities, if they think they are not smart and if they hate to write or think they can't spell—that's what their schooling taught them—that is what they learned in school.

18. *School is the way it is because those in charge through the years made it that way and those now in charge are the only ones who can change it.* Unfortunately, those in charge of education have a vested interest in not changing schools. For them, schooling was at least successful enough that they graduated from college and chose to become a part. They have difficulty comprehending what school was like for the dropouts and force-outs; for the psychological dropouts: those who merely tolerate the classes; and for those who remember little more than friends and social aspects of their schooling. Most of all they cannot visualize what learning kids were missing or failing to experience while they were forced passively or reluctantly to "play the school game."

141

19. *Schooling as we have all experienced it is obsolete.* The educational bureaucracy has never been able to keep up with a changing society. Now, with individual access to information, improved technology, and increased mobility, anyone can learn anything that school teaches, anytime she chooses, efficiently and effectively without the bureaucracy. People, including students, have become empowered through television (especially video tapes) computers and the internet. Improvements and options are increasing exponentially and continuously for each person.

20. *Even a hasty perusal of demographics shows the need for change in direction as well as change in education.* If society had not become so violent; if family values had not eroded; if society could tolerate non-productive, illiterate, citizens; if we could provide a welfare society; we could continue our current educational processes by improving or upgrading the system. But, the system can't be "fixed"; it must be changed.

21. *Society has the right to decide what society shall be.* (Given laws of nature, human nature, some inalienable rights, and a bill of rights.) Society must create new ways of thinking, of existing, and of acting. Emphasis must be on learning not on teaching; on the learner, not on the teacher; and, on better ways of providing and mediating experiences, not on better schooling.

22. *Kids develop identities.* They adopt the behaviors, symbols, labels and characteristics, from subtle to ostentatious, that

142

identify "who he is." While he has multiple identities with labels such as a goody-goody, rebel, tough guy, jock, nerd, teacher's pet, or egghead it is the primary or over-riding identity such as a "stereotypical cowboy" that tends to direct the preponderance of his or her experiences—hat, boots, belt buckle, adornments, rodeos, Skoal, pick-up truck, slang, twang, music, mannerisms, interests, and so on.

23. *The Pygmalion principal can skew the experiences that shape kids lives.* In George Bernard Shaw's Pygmalion he states, "A lady is a lady, not because of how she acts; but because of how she's treated." Once a kid is labeled bad, dumb, nerd, or slob she is on her way to having it become official; and without significant intervention, become permanent.

24. *"A Child's life is like a piece of paper on which every person leaves a mark." (Chinese Proverb)* Kids are never not learning. They learn what they experience and they are always experiencing something. Adults have little direct or intentional control over most experiences. They simply "happen" in the course of living their lives. In the first five years of kids' lives, they learn more than they are likely to learn in any other period of time. They master an entire language, they build a 10,000-word vocabulary, and they learn about most everything in their lives.

With their entry into school, it is though they can't be trusted to continue learning. Now they must be required to learn, motivated to learn, forced into preplanned experiences. Why couldn't the second five years of life be like the first five years? The answer is because we feel the need to manage or control their learning according to our desires, plans, and schedules.

Let's Begin with a Few Questions

Why not begin with the questions, "What do we want our kids to be? What do we want them to be like? What do we want them to value, appreciate, and know? What rules and limits to we think they need? After answering these questions, we need only ask, "What experiences can we offer that will enable kids to go right on learning as they always have?"

Here's a question to answer right now, "Why is it that human nature and children's early learning are so contrary to school's learning policies and teaching procedures?"

My Teaching Credo

> *"My beliefs determine my actions. To improve my teaching, I first examine my beliefs. I reconcile my teaching procedures with my beliefs about how children learn, and I declare publicly my personal credo against which all my teaching behavior can be evaluated."*

Through my years of teaching, I developed a written set of personal beliefs about my responsibilities as a professional teacher. I found that those beliefs became more meaningful when personalized into a specific creed. I use this creed to reflect on and to critique my teaching. I explain my credo, its intent, and my goals to my students. I invite students to critique my teaching based on my declarations and use this credo as a "Student Bill of Rights."

I. I hereby guarantee: that I will:

✓ Utilize democratic principles as the basis of my relationship and interaction with all students.

✓ Provide each student with a student-centered learning continuum that invites learning by individual discovery and inquiry.

✓ Provide each student with equal access to learning experiences appropriate to his or her needs.

II. I shall strive to use, offer, or provide the following:

✓ Production-driven, thematic, concept, hands-on, cooperative, teaching strategies, and procedures.

✓ Independent study and learning options.

✓ Learning experiences determined by, or cooperatively with, the personal needs and interests of each learner.

✓ Creative learning processes through discovery, exploration, collaboration, and inquiry.

✓ Learning experiences as a single entity (without regard to curricula categories) with emphasis on communication (speaking, listening, reading, and writing).

✓ Field trips as an integral, ongoing, regular, frequent, small group activity.

✓ Student exchange, student cooperation, student interaction.

✓ Inter-school and inter-district student cooperation, collaboration, and exchange.

✓ Community resources as a broad, expansive, convenient experience resource.

III. I shall make special effort to:

✓ Develop and insure democratic relationships through modeling, interpersonal skills, values, and experiences.

✓ Encourage areas of study that reflect ethnic, cultural, and individual interests.

✓ Encourage interest in, and examination of, contemporary issues.

✓ Be cognizant of the potential for many kinds of biases, prejudices, and discrimination on my part and to critique myself regularly to reduce that potential and possibility.

✓ Create and develop quality learning experiences for and with each student.

IV. I shall abandon, abolish, eliminate, and fight the use of the following:

✓ The feeling of constraints caused by the length of the school day, week, or year.

✓ Formal examinations except at the student's request for his or her own use and benefit.

✓ Assigned "homework" (replaced with projects that encourage cooperation, independent study, and personal relevance and interest.)

✓ The idea of discipline as separate from learning, responsibility, or communication.

✓ The use of class rank, percentage marks, letter grades, norm standards, or grading (replaced by authentic, holistic, student-involved assessment, and by portfolios, student work, exhibits, and a standard of "personal best").

THIS CREDO IS TO BE POSTED PROMINENTLY AND MADE AVAILABLE TO STUDENTS, THEIR PARENTS, VISITORS, AND OTHER INTERESTED PARTIES.

My credo is an integral, summative, applied part of my beliefs, experiences, knowledge, and ability, all of which have grown, developed, and changed during more than four decades of teaching. Once I started developing the concept of "building a democratic community of learners" as the essence of classroom teaching-learning relationships; and once students experienced the responsibility and freedom of a participatory classroom, techniques, learning and collaboration, cooperative learning relationships developed and progressed in the classroom at an exponential rate.

When a credo is written and declared publicly, it serves as a "stake in the ground,"—a point from which professional and personal growth can be measured, developed, and assessed. A Credo serves to promote growth and movement toward greater effectiveness as a professional educator. This credo has changed, improved, and progresses through many stages of adjustment, revision, and through years of use.

Teachers Are Individuals Too

Teacher individuality is unfortunate. It messes up a lot of standardized teaching, direct instruction, classroom management strategies, and unrealistic mandates of politicians and bureaucrats who have no idea what teachers actually do

With her long, braided pigtails, effervescent personality, and permanent, pixie smile, I couldn't help thinking of Trish as a "girl," not as the fine professional teacher she was. Trish weighed scarcely 87 pounds and was all of five feet tall. She was 25 years old, married, and had four years teaching experience. I was certain she could go through any elementary school lunch line, pay student prices, and never be challenged.

Trish had been designated teacher of a research project in her school. The project, which I headed, involved eight inner city junior high schools in the worst poverty core of Nashville. Trish's school, one of two among the eight schools, widely known as "white ghetto schools," experienced large numbers of students commonly referred to as "trailer-trash," "rednecks," "glue-sniffers," and "freaks." These labels, some students called each other and seemed proud of the designation. The eight schools identified their lowest-achieving incoming seventh-graders without regard to the reason for the low achievement. The research premise postulated teachers' need to "change teaching procedures rather than focusing student problems."

What Would You Do With That Kid?

One day, as I visited Trish with her 30 "troublemakers," she questioned, "Well, what would you do with that kid?" That kid being Tyrone, a lanky, tough-looking, muscular, seventh-grader who was two years over-age, two feet over-tall and had served two six-month hitches at Jordonia Juvenile Facility. She described a recent incident in which Tyrone had attacked a younger, smaller classmate. "It wasn't a typical scuffle," she assured me. "It was a one-sided beating. I thought Tyrone was trying to kill Anthony."

A Definitive Answer

My response to Trish's question was instantaneous. "I would quickly grab Tyrone by the shirt collar, ram my knuckle in his Adam's apple, and thrust my legs behind his legs, jerking him to the floor. Kneeling with my knee and full weight on his back and my knuckle now painfully into the back of his neck, I would press his head and nose hard against the floor, until I could reason with him." Her shocked, flabbergasted retort was, "I couldn't do that!"

To which I replied, "You didn't ask what you should do, you asked what I would do; and that's exactly what I would do." I weigh 300 pounds, played college football, served two years in the army, where I took a course in hand-to-hand combat. I have never seen a junior high student I can't handle, or manhandle if necessary for the safety of my students. I'm sure there are some, but I haven't met one yet.

I Don't Know What You Should Do?

I don't know what I would do if I were an 87-pound woman. I've never been an 87-pound woman; it has been since fifth grade that I was an 87-pound boy. If my goal were to prevent a murder, I would do whatever was necessary. "I have no idea how someone like you would react in those circumstances," I explained to Trish.

"I don't know if you should run down the hall screaming for help? Flee to the next teacher's room? Open the window and shout "Rape?" Demand that some classmates' help subdue Tyrone? Pick up a chair and whack him across the back? Push the intercom button? Cry? Plead? Scream? Ponder? Pray? (Oops, that's not allowed!) I really don't know."

Incidentally, I learned that at the time of the clash, Trish had run out of the room to find Dr. Dunkerly, a shaved-headed, pro-wrestler-looking assistant principal, apparently chosen for skills, and perhaps size, in dealing with the population of that particular school. By the time "Mr. Clean" and Trish returned, Tyrone was sitting on Anthony. With his arm twisted behind his back, Anthony was screaming, pleading for mercy, and crying in pain.

Teacher training institutions act as though all teachers have the same abilities, same communication skills, same personalities, same demeanor, same tolerance for noise, and assume they all have the same temperament and competencies. Somehow in teacher training, those in charge, forget to allow for individual differences in teachers.

A Sad Milestone

I remember a sad moment in my twentieth year of teaching when it really hit home to me that the school system did not regard me any differently at that point in my career than when I was a first-year teacher. I had the same number of students, the same amount of preparation time, the same supervision, the same number of meetings, memos, policies, and procedures. I can teach 500 students now better than I could teach the 32 they gave me back when I started—but every teacher gets 25 students per class whether she is a first-year teacher or a 40-year teacher.

I'll Decide What I Do

A skilled worker does not rely on a bag of tricks. A professional looks at the desired outcome and determines what tools or techniques will be needed and which ones are available to him. Of course, a big box of tools and ample resources are helpful, but we, as teachers, need to draw on their personal style, strengths, personalities, and resources, not on predetermined techniques that presume "one size fits all."

An old maxim states, "If you know enough to distinguish good advice from bad advice, you don't need the advice." I don't need teaching advice. Just tell me what you would do or how you see the situation. I'll decide whether to adopt, adapt, or reject your reasoning. I can then decide what else I might do or whom else I might ask for advice.

Too Bad Humans are Involved

There is one major, over-riding, constant problem with teaching: it involves human beings. The students, parents, teachers, and administrators are each and every one human. If they were not, we could apply the same procedures to all of them and expect them all to respond alike. Besides the human factor, individual teaching conditions prohibit standardized procedures.

Come to think of it, different people, with different perceptions in different circumstances is really good news. Who would want all students to be alike, every teacher to teach the same, and teaching procedures standardized?

What is Your Goal?

If possible, would we want every student on the honor roll, and if so, would there not be concern for those at the bottom of the honor roll? Even if every student were on the top of the honor roll, wouldn't there be concern for those who took longer to get there, struggled to make it, or had "other" deficiencies, such as in behavior, social skills, attitude, or other obstacle? Would there be a need or interest in the honor roll if every student were at the top? If we could, would we have every student graduate from college? Graduate with honors? From graduate school? What goals do you think are worthwhile?

I find myself pondering, "If schools were really effective, what would students who come from them be like?" I fear we would have a bunch of "well-rounded" individuals who know a little bit of history and a little bit of science, a little bit of music, and a little bit of art. They would all have read the same books, memorized the same poems, and scored a hundred on the standardized tests. Oh, for an educational cookie cutter!

Comparative Physical Fitness

I remember when my older daughter, attending junior high, came home with a physical education report based on a national fitness test (AHPER, or American Health and Physical Education Rating), comparing abilities in physical tasks such as pull-ups, push-ups, sit-ups, and at least two other tasks. As I recall, in the percentile rankings, she had one score of 38, with remaining scores even lower. As my wife lamented the "miserable showing," I asked if she would like to have our daughter initiate a fitness regimen hoping to raise her ranking so someone else's child could rank 38th? When rank ordering a hundred individuals, aren't some going to rank high and some low? Is everyone expected to be above average in everything—aaahh, Lake Woebegone Rules?

I Thought I'd Never Reach Average Teacher Pay

I remember my first teaching contract 44 years ago, which with two steps on the salary scale for military service, called for an annual salary of $4,600. That amount far exceeded the starting teacher pay in all but two of St. Louis County's 27 school districts and considerably higher than the surrounding counties. Although I started with a high salary, it became evident to me that I would never receive "average teacher pay," because every year as my pay increased, by a yearly increment, so did the pay of those getting average salary. Were it not for the top paid teachers retiring and new teachers coming in, I could never have made it to average pay.

I'm Glad I'm Different

I admire those who enjoy communicating with computers, dealing with technology and mastering electronic gadgets. I'm glad there are the accountant type personalities who can figure their own income tax and are willing to do mine (for a fee, of course). I'm pleased there are people who are content working in grease or blood up to their elbows. My school failed in its efforts to make me into what it thought I should be, and I'm glad it failed. By utilizing my strengths, I became a unique, successful teacher.

I'm happy nobody in my career path demanded or even expected me to be a proctologist, a funeral director, a debt collector, a prison guard, or thousands of other occupations, careers, or professions I could name. I'm glad humans are all different. I'm glad I am different. I like being different. I like being me. I like me!

Marching to a Different Paradigm

Student Achievement via Teacher Effectiveness

Ever since the rising tide of mediocre reports reminded us that our nation was at risk, there has been a continuous, intense, prolonged flurry of activity designed to reform the education system. The reports further reminded us that schools are, and should be, our best hope, in the long run, for dealing with societal ills including drugs, violence, crime, poverty, and discrimination.

Schools can change only when and to the extent that teachers change. Teachers do the work of education; they are the heart and soul of education. Learning occurs or fails to occur in each classroom. The increased achievement we seek will happen to each student and involve each teacher in each classroom.

In the middle, between state standards and standardized testing is the teacher. The demand is for every student to learn the mandated curricula, but there cannot be improvement in student achievement without a corresponding improvement in teacher effectiveness. If teachers taught more, kids would learn more. If teachers taught individually, kids would learn individually. It all boils down to the relationship between teachers' teaching and learners' learning.

New Demands Require a New Paradigm

While the best measure of success is student achievement, the only route to success is teacher effectiveness. And, increased teacher effectiveness is via professional development. We must measure, evaluate, and judge the improved learning by student achievement. This new mandate requires new teaching strategies and a new paradigm that fully acknowledges the interdependence of the teaching-learning relationship while respecting the independence of both the teacher and the student. To construct her own knowledge, students must have ownership of her knowledge, learning, and experiences. Teachers are essentially "students" of their own students, one responsible for studying and learning what and how to "tune in to and plug into" the students' learning experiences. Teaching is the "use" of knowledge based on understanding and interacting appropriately and strategically with each learner.

"The Interdependent Paradigm"

The teaching relationship requires that both the student and the teacher, through his or her independence, choose to work together, to cooperate, working interdependently. Teaching is the teacher functioning as a facilitator not as a taskmaster. It is like creating a hybrid, a third set of options not created by either, but created jointly through the interaction and interrelation of two separate viewpoints. The teaching process is the voluntary, mutual interacting that enables both parties to move toward high achievement goals, while sustain high energy and maximizing the teaching-learning relationship. Administrators can utilize this interdependent paradigm in their own relationships and for increasing teacher understanding of a better relationship that can increase student achievement and move toward improved effectiveness.

Four Strands

The interdependent paradigm involves a better understanding of the role of teacher-student relationship, attitude, responsibility and learning community. The paradigm offers four strands through which teachers can improve effectiveness and move toward closing the achievement gap for all kids, including those most at risk, while maintaining and improving the achievement level of the remainder of the students. The four strands of the interdependent paradigm are these:

1. Toward self-critique, self-assessment and self-reflection

2. Toward an inner locus of control

3. Toward utilizing and emphasizing teaching strategies

4. Toward leadership that encourages the new paradigm

1. Self-Reflection—Toward teacher self-critique, self-assessment, and self-reflection.

Individual change is the function of choice, belief, and commitment. I am the only person in the world who can change me. Individuals don't resist change—what they resist is being changed. Rules and mandates can coerce me into compliance, but the change necessary to increase the achievement of the kids, especially those at the bottom, is far beyond compliance. Initiation of action is required, not merely responsiveness to rules.

One way to help teachers change themselves is through self-reflection. Self-reflection is looking at a kind of mirror image of ourselves. It involves gathering information about ourselves and focusing on seeing our teaching behaviors as others see them. It requires critique—looking at positives and negatives. It requires systematic, ongoing, repeated assessment; and it requires specific goals chosen by the teacher himself with help from peers and instructional leaders of his choice. It might involve videotaping, student feedback, friend or colleague observation, or administrative consultation. If teachers want to teach better and believe they can teach better, they request and welcome feedback, even when it is negative.

There are many excellent examples of reflective practices, and sufficient research in the current educational literature to help teachers move toward self-evaluation, identifying strengths and weaknesses, and improving skills and repertoire for teachers to begin the process through peer collaboration, review, and mentoring. Each teacher, with help from his or her peers and individual leaders, can improve his or her ability to increase student achievement. The only thing or person that can move me toward excellence is I, and, I could sure use some help.

The same is true of school districts; only the district can move itself toward excellence and improved attitude. Mandates or state departments cannot make a district excellent. They might bring compliance, but only district leaders can bring about excellence. It is through self-critique that the district can improve. And the same is true for students—each of them.

2. Pro-Active Choices—Toward an inner locus of control.

Some teachers believe their behavior, attitude, and feelings are controlled by random, circumstantial, or outside forces. They believe that whether they have a good day or bad day depends on how the kids behave, the weather, their colleagues, society, parents, and other factors. They are "outer" controlled. Other teachers are "inner" controlled. They are pro-active; they choose whether they have a good day, regardless of how kids or others behave. They take responsibility for their actions.

If teachers believe students don't learn because their parents won't discipline them; or believe they watch too much TV; then, until their parents change or turn off the TV, they think they can't teach him. But if teachers believe they can get them out of their desks moving instead of complaining about their wiggling, or come in with a smile instead of a frown, they can control the learning.

To be effective with at-risk kids, teachers must be pro-active not reactive. They must move toward seeing that they have control over their feelings, attitudes, and behaviors in relation to the "bottom" kids. Through taking charge of their own feelings, teachers can make a difference in the success of the problem learners; indeed, the teachers are probably the only ones who can! Teachers need help to feel in control and learn to make pro-active choices. Whether I have a good day or an interesting class depends on me not on my students.

3. Authentic Learning—Utilizing and emphasizing teaching strategies that capture all kids' interest, enthusiasm, and involvement, making at-risk kids an integral part of the classroom.

Teachers have the obligation to make their classes interesting and appropriate to each student. Teachers are the only ones who can. Parents, administrators, and texts do not determine whether a class is boring or inappropriate. Kids do not determine whether a class is exciting or relevant.

Groups do not learn. Only individuals (in a group, perhaps) learn. If 58% of the group learned, we might say "they learned," but they didn't. Each individual in the group either did or did not learn. The teaching strategies must enable each student to learn.

A class science project of building a 6-foot papier-mâché insect enables students to cooperate with one another doing different jobs within their capability and interest. The research, discussion, collaboration, decisions, problem solving, and satisfaction or the project involves cooperation within a community of learners and individual learning in the group. The following are some strategies teachers might use to make classes appropriate to all students:

- Authentic learning
- Collaborative learning
- Contextual learning
- Production-driven activities
- Problem-based learning
- Hands-on activities
- Project approach
- Thematic units
- Concept approach
- Self-directed learning

4. Administrative Encouragement—Toward leadership that encourages the new paradigm.

Teacher performance, conformity, and compliance. To evaluate my teaching, don't observe me, observe my kids; see what they are doing or learning. Observe and question whether my students are excited, involved, engaged, cooperating, working independently; ask them to tell you what they are learning, how and why they are learning. They can tell you. And, don't use the Hunter Model teaching checklist to observe me when I'm using the inquiry or discovery approach. Have the pre- and post-observation conferences with my students, not me and be prepared to answer their questions about state standards, standardized testing, relevance, and about the "whys" for which they see no reasons.

Administrators cannot make teachers change or improve. No one can make anyone else improve. If they could have, they would have done it long ago. At-risk kids can improve, but not by any of the methods that have already failed us. Some compliance is, of course necessary; but it cannot close the achievement gap. Only each student with each teacher can do that for himself or herself. Administrators can support, direct, guide, and encourage that relationship and interaction.

Moving toward self-reflection, pro-active choices, authentic learning activities, and appropriate administrative support are necessary procedures for increasing student achievement. And they all necessitate voluntary cooperation so that each student and each teacher in each classroom will learn. That is the interdependent paradigm.

School Learning Occurs In School

Kids have learned, can learn, do learn, and will learn all their lives. But the learning that schools value, test and report on occurs or fails to occur to each student, with each teacher in each classroom.

While kids learn continuously throughout life in many ways and from many sources, the learning for which schools are responsible and accountable occurs in school. Furthermore, that learning occurs or fails to occur to each student with each teacher in each classroom and is the direct result of the continuous, moment-to-moment, day-by-day interaction between teachers and students.

Teachers may assign interactive work student-to-student, or between a student and computers, workbooks, videos, and work at home. But it is the planned experiences, assigned and supervised by teachers that constitute school learning. Purportedly measured by the T-CAP, TAKS, FCAT, CASE, WASL, and other "alphabet soup" tests mandated by politicians in the "No Child Left Behind (or untested) Act," school learning is presumably the only product of the education system that matters in the school authorities' quest for accountability.

Teachers Do the Work of Education

If the function of school is learning, and school learning occurs in school classrooms through interaction with teachers, then teachers are the heart and soul of student learning—they do the real work of education. To the kids, teachers are school; to parents and society better teaching is the answer to quality education. The purpose of school is student learning. Students learn through continuous interaction with teachers. Anyone hired by the school who doesn't interact with students is unnecessary, unless they cause better interaction to occur in the classrooms.

To do their job, teachers need bus drivers to transport kids to school, cafeteria staff to prepare and serve mid-day nutrition, custodial staff to provide clean, safe facilities, and administrators (maybe not nearly as many as the school board seems to think) to administer the available educational resources. The classified school personnel's contribution to the schooling process is obvious because it is observable and sensible. Not so obvious is what principals and district administrators contribute to increase student achievement, especially for at-risk students. Problem learners continue to plague teachers until they dropout and plague society.

A Role Change for Administrators

Under the dictates of the federal No Child Left Behind Act, state governments, national testing companies, college academicians, textbook profiteers, budget priorities, politicians, local bureaucracies, "bottom-line" business interests, lay boards of education, high-priced school district directors, private tutoring firms, and intimidated principals, education priorities have changed. Schools, teachers, and students must submit to "exit poll type tests" at the end of each year. The results of a few hours of testing will now measure, rank, compare, publicize and label more than 1200 hours of school experiences—a school year of student-teacher interaction results measured by a few hours of fill-in-the-bubble-testing. All of this changes the principals' roles significantly.

In the "good old days" of frequent new programs and innovations by the numbers, with each year bringing a new reform plan, teachers could hide away in their rooms, close the door, tape paper over the window of the door, do "their thing," bide their time and be reasonably sure that before long, "this too shall pass." The foolproof high-stakes "gotcha" tests now render these once safe, reliable avoidance practices useless. Newspapers report student scores and ranking. Schools are rated and labeled.

Now principals are held accountable for the overall test scores and for student improvement. They are expected to reorder their priorities, putting instructional leadership as job number one, while functioning as the school administrator. For years principals were trained to administer schools and to function as school managers. In the late 1980s, their new role as instructional leaders began gaining favor and was included to some extent in principal training. It is only recently that the journals and colleges have shown any real interest in the new role.

Four Serious New Problems

Of the many problems with which teachers and principals currently deal, time to teach is the greatest. Having been usurped by four culprits that deprive them of their precious teaching time, teachers have had to reorder their priorities in ways that reduce their effectiveness. While many teachers would want to include paperwork, meetings, hostile attitudes of parents and student disrespect, lack of student self-discipline, direct instruction programs, bureaucratic intrusion, and lack of parental involvement, the root of the most serious classroom problems are these:

1. "The test" is the determiner of curriculum, teaching procedures, priorities, time, and effort. Whether the tests are valid, whether they succeed or fail to measure what they purport to measure, whether what they measure is of any real value, whether their numbers are statistically useful to anyone, whether they are biased, whether the assessment information is worth billions of dollars, and particularly, whether small percentage increases and decreases in achievement in a given school are meaningful or significant and whether the improvement will hold the next year makes no difference—tests are the primary influence in education today.

2. Closing the huge, persistent achievement gap, whether the gap is between ethnicities, races, cultures, economic classes, at-risk students, and gender groups. Whatever the basis of the gap, students feel the devastating effects of being on the bottom of the, "raising the bar" movement; "high stakes testing," requirements, while continuing the winner-loser and passing-failing classifications, the grading and rankings of students, classes and schools, are persistent problems— problems for which no answer is considered, much less offered by those in charge.

3. The students obviously left behind in the "No Child Left Behind Act," including increased dropouts, grade repeaters, force-outs, psychological dropouts, disengaged, GED-seekers; summer schoolers, (including those who fail there too), English-as-a-second-language kids, "special ed" students, cheating teachers and "stay-at-home-on-test-day" kids, leave a lot of questions about what is meant by "left behind." For the thousands upon thousands of children flunked for the year (40,000 retained in the third grade just in the state of Florida) and those denied graduation and diplomas, their lives are forever changed. Perhaps the law should be called the No Child Left Unharmed Act.

4. Instead of resources, respect, time, encouragement and autonomy, teachers get teacher-proof lesson nonsense, political intrusion, anxiety, constant pressure, and direct instruction materials. What is not being taught, mountains of paperwork from over size class loads, bureaucratic infringement and from the higher-ups who don't trust teachers to do their jobs has replaced the student-teacher relationships that form the basis of the teaching learning process.

Fortunately, teachers get their meaningful feedback from individual students who learn, improve, change, and become more confident. Teachers see kids develop and know they have made a difference, regardless of the evaluation methods chosen by the school system or the state. But, they themselves are treated like children.

Student Achievement Equals Teacher Effectiveness

Kids' achievement will increase when teachers improve their teaching effectiveness. But how are teachers to improve? Why will teachers be more effective this school year than they were last year? What is it that would or could make any difference? What do staff development directors offer other than intimidation by assessment, coercion to improve student achievement, increase teacher accountability, and label and rank schools? We cannot expect improved student achievement without a corresponding increase in teacher effectiveness. And we cannot expect increased teacher effectiveness without lots of help and many changes. The "Leave No Child Behind" movement (which thus far appears to be a "Leave No Child Untested" or "Leave No Profiteering Corporation Unpaid" movement) must begin with classroom teachers, not because teachers are the problem, but because teachers are the solution.

The keys to improving teacher effectiveness are: first, teacher empowerment through increased participation, time, reflection, collaboration, and responsibility for improving their own knowledge, skills, and competence. Second, the principal of the school should be responsible for staff development in her building by leading, organizing, mentoring, coaching, and directing improvement efforts in individual teachers and within individual classrooms.

Now, the recent movement toward embedded, continuous, ongoing responsibility for staff development really makes even more sense. The principal knows the teachers better than anyone else in the school system, is with them on a daily basis, knows most about what is happening, cares about every kid and every family; knows what is important in the school and community, and is responsible for observing, evaluating, supporting and improving teacher performance. The principal is responsible for the climate, morale, teamwork, and culture of the school. The principal makes a significant difference, for better or worse, in the school's success.

Teachers Don't Just MAKE a Difference, They ARE the Difference

Teacher control and influence over the most basic aspects of education have not changed in the past century. Teachers have no control over the external conditions; which room, which students, which curriculum, textbooks, resource allocations, prior learning conditions, school policies and procedures, colleagues, schedules, time allocation, parental involvement, special services, budget factors, district rules, school personnel, and so forth.

Although teachers make instructional decisions and constant choices within the teacher-student interaction, increasingly teachers are more restricted by mandatory programs, core curriculum, assessment policies, direct teaching programs, and the intrusion of additional lessons in character training, conflict resolution, AIDS prevention, and the dozens of political inclusions in the curriculum. All this notwithstanding, teachers do make choices and non-choices that make the difference in what, how and whether students improve their achievement. They can only hope the "fill in the bubble," "multiple guess" tests will reflect some of the increased achievement to which they alone know they have contributed.

Empowering Teachers

Because of teachers' increased accountability for student achievement, they must be empowered to change their teaching procedures and their classroom techniques and activities. That is the only part within the teacher's control. Schools can change only when and to the extent that teachers change. Teachers do the work of education; they are the difference in increased student achievement and improved test scores. More than anyone else, they understand the needs and priorities of the classroom. Teachers know their students better than any one else in the school system possibly could. There is a difference and knowing about a kid, as the system might determine; and knowing the kid as teachers does. Teachers need autonomy in their classrooms to make the decisions about student learning—not because they can do it best—but because they are the only ones who can do it at all.

School Learning Occurs in School

School learning occurs in school. It requires that teachers help each kid, in each classroom learn the prescribed curriculum for each subject. It further requires that the principal provide helpful policies, ongoing, embedded staff development, that other staff members on the periphery do their job. Having spent 180 days or class meetings with their students, teachers know their students; they know their achievement and their progress. All that teachers need at that point is an effective way of reporting that achievement on a report card and school record.

Whether others who are interested in teacher effectiveness and student achievement, know which students have learned, what they have learned and at what level of proficiency, is their problem. How the achievement is measured, evaluated, and reported by those other than the kid's teacher, is expensive, time consuming, confusing, and problematic. Their attempt at "intimidation by testing" in effort to make it the teacher's problem and to find a meaningful, statistical average is unfortunate, unproductive, and unfair. Its total effect is equivalent to holding a loaded gun to each teacher's head and saying, "Do better or else." Pray tell, what good is that?

My Reaction to a School Incident
Reported in the St. Louis Post-Dispatch

My sister, who still lives in Missouri where I started my teaching career, sends me educational news clippings from the St. Louis newspaper. Vashon High School is in the heart of the worst ghetto area of St Louis. The new, forty-million-dollar, politically inspired, state-of-the-art building was built to replace the old Vashon High that was demolished.

Vashon's problems made two major stories with half-page size pictures of kids fighting in the halls, and a full-page story of broken furniture, criticism, blame, and a plea to "call out the National Guard." Of the 1580 students enrolled, fewer than 1000 attend on any given day. One newspaper columnist told of his high school days and thought fighting in high school is ordinary. In a follow-up second column he described a walk in the Vashon neighborhood and blamed those conditions for Vashon's problems. There were six letters to the editor with the usual diatribe.

173

I decided to write a response. I sent it to the columnist. Here it is:

Hallway Problems At Vashon High

Maybe Problems Are Really Just Symptoms

Two categories of possibilities for eliminating the problems of the "mobs of kids" in the Vashon hallways are these: First, get a "Joe Clark," with his eardrum shattering bullhorn, his menacing baseball bat and his "final solution" huge pad of suspension/expulsion forms and follow his procedures in the movie "Lean On Me." Second, provide worthwhile activities, appropriate studies and content levels, study help, student participation and involvement, and meaningful hands-on material in the classrooms. Perhaps the hall marauders and the 500 plus absentee students are manifestations of the problem, not the problem.

With sufficient power to clear the halls and ability to intimidate those who stay, authorities, especially with the aid of uniformed police, iron gates, metal detectors, and baton-wielding hall monitors, could rid the halls of the menaces, while the suspended students hang on street corners, parking lots, and at convenience markets. These students and their counterparts, who do go to class and do nothing while there, are never powerless. They are simply forced to use their power in perverse and defiant ways. Thus it is possible for schools to get rid of the miscreants as someone else's problem, and coerce school conformity on those remaining. Such methods can get perfunctory compliance, but they will also to get resentment, defiance, violence, passive aggression, vandalism and apathy both in and out of school in both student groups.

Vashon High, a 40 million dollar, year-old school, has no real value to those who cannot partake meaningfully of its lessons or profit from its offerings. Alienated, marginalized, defeated, "at-risk," and disengaged students have no stake in the beautiful facility, its teachers, its teachings, its activities or its successful students. Can there be any question on the basis of the hall rovers past performance, academic record, testing (both standardized and classroom), teacher testimony, or their own admission, whether these "trouble makers" lack the ability to utilize the courses being offered? One cannot expect chronic losers (after nine years in school, already) to like or cooperate with the game rules, the winners, or the game officials.

Before the authorities condemn the students' behavior, perhaps they should consider what is being required. Most assuredly, the high school curriculum is inappropriate for a significant number of students because of their reading ability, attitude, past performance and prerequisite knowledge; so they act as though it is inappropriate. The school personnel in turn act as though there is something wrong with the students instead of accepting student behavior as valid feedback reflecting on the school offerings from a student perspective. This would answer the question of what is appropriate, with regard to the subjects, materials, difficulty level, and usefulness.

Students are always interested in aspects of their lives that most affect them, that impinge upon them and cause them pain or satisfaction. If schools offered courses in interpersonal relations; how to get along with parents, siblings and friends: male/female relationships; non-violent communication; self-improvement; and how to make money (not a "School to Work" course). Has anyone ask the students what they want or how they see it? Given worthwhile subjects, students would flock to the classes and the problem would be getting them to leave.

Those in charge should examine what they need to do, what they may be doing wrong, and what they can change before looking at what the students are doing wrong and what students must change? Shall the school deal with the problem or deal with the symptoms? That is the first question to be answered.

With joy in sharing, Bill Page

A Great Model of Differentiation

To find motivated kids, individualized learning, success with kids at-risk and differentiation too—check out the extra-curricular programs.

So long as teachers rely on singular lessons and assignment for the class, and so long as they control the step-by-step learning procedures through assignments, worksheets, evaluation, grading, and homework, students must necessarily be treated in groups and thereby every student treated pretty much alike according to the needs of the group, regardless of individual differences in prior learning, interests, abilities, and needs. For teachers, the only alternative to teaching students in a group is teaching them as individuals; conversely, the only alternative to individualizing is grouping. Short of complete one-on-one individualization, teachers have only the choice of what the size and criteria of the grouping will be.

Learning is Constructed by Each Student

Learning is a personal, individual experience that is constructed within the unique perceptions and experiences of each student. Every group has individuals of differing personalities, learning styles, emotions, and backgrounds; but, since a one-to-one ratio of teacher to student is not practical in classrooms, schools must, of necessity, group students in classes. One way to move toward teaching individuals is by differentiation. Teachers who differentiate usually do so in the three major areas of a lesson plan: (1) Procedures, (2), Assignments, and (3) Assessments, regarding each area as a separate entity.

Teaching Individuals in a Group

Technically, teachers cannot teach a class; they teach individuals in a class. Consideration should, therefore, be given to ways to individualize learning for each student within a group of learners. By far, the best examples of individualization elements include diversity, self-directed learning, inclusion, peer coaching, cooperation, mentoring, and ethnic sensitivity can be found in out-of-school activities and in-school extra-curricular activities. In these settings, ranging from little league, scouts, school athletic teams, and ballet classes to chess clubs and FFA (Future Farmers of America), kids of all ages, abilities, and backgrounds can come together; can function meaningfully, learn according to personal interest, desire and capability, and enjoy the activities as individuals in the group of diverse learners. With a stated purpose, understood goals and

178

clear by-laws the group easily operates without school-like reward-punishment and discipline problems and coercion.

Individualizing in Sports

I have always marveled that a high school coach can takes 60 or more students who range from 78-pound freshmen to 300-pound seniors, from new team members who don't know how to put on a uniform, to three-year varsity lettermen and without an assistant, report cards, attendance officer, or fear-based supervision, teach young teenagers to play football at a high skill, high inter-scholastic competitive level. And, amazingly, brings on new members to replace the loss of the best players each year, while maintaining team integrity. Understanding what is involved and how this is done is an important key to complete classroom differentiation.

Characteristics of Extra-Curricular Activities

Some of the many characteristics of away-from-school organizations or extra-curricular success with widely diverse individuals important to adopting fully differentiated, cooperative, and individualized learning in regular classrooms are the following:

A COMMON GOAL: To win a game, present a program, or produce a play, requires that each member contribute his/her share toward the goals and objectives. Some students may be stars and some may be benchwarmers, but all do their part to the best of their ability in cooperation and collaboration with others on the team and with a coach or resource person coordinating efforts to reach the common goals. Each knows the goal and contributes to it. Reaching the goal requires everyone doing his/her part. Such is life.

MEANINGFUL ACTIVITY: Members of the group see reasons for their input and for the rules and the discipline necessary to accomplish the agreed group activities or projects. They also realize that everyone's role, however small, is important and each takes individual responsibility for his or her contribution.

COOPERATION: Team members work together, learn from one another, collaborate, give, and accept feedback and evaluation, they function according to their own abilities, strengths, and interests. Except when occasionally vying for the same position, students do not compete with each other. For the good of the group, they willingly help each other to succeed. They take pleasure in sharing; in seeing their colleagues learn, improving, succeeding, and becoming more proficient.

SATISFACTION: What is known as the three P's—performance, production, and product (not necessarily a tangible product)—all contribute to the morale, spirit, self-worth, and pride. The feeling of team accomplishments, successes, publicity, and recognition are shared by each and every participant regardless of the magnitude his or her role and contribution.

MORALE: Successful coaches know that fundamentals of the game are essential. The difference in winning or improving, however, is the team morale, esprit de corps, and camaraderie. That is why we have cheerleaders, pep talks, and enjoyment mixed with the hard work of practice, preparation, and accomplishment. Learning math is not just a matter of learning the basics; it involves an attitude with the satisfaction of knowing, participating, cooperating, and accomplishing.

RELATIONSHIP TO THE LEADER: The leaders of teams and organizations both in and out of school are most frequently referred to as coach or sponsor, not teacher. And for good reason, she is there as a helper, or resource, the one on whom they rely to share their expertise, goals, procedures, and feedback to the endeavor. She does not need report cards, phone calls to parents, or a handy principal's office. She derives his position or authority by virtue of her knowledge; supervision role, her resourcefulness, and ability to assist students in acquiring important knowledge and skills. If the goal is to produce a school newspaper, the one who knows most about it offers advice and gives guidance, critique, and leadership to produce a product to which each participant can be proud to have contributed.

VARIETY OF ACTIVITIES: To create a product or present a performance, there are many phases to the process, many levels of activities and skills, and need for a variety of personal skills and abilities. A football coach does not need all players with big stereotype football builds to field a football team. It is best to have big husky linemen, quick small scat backs, tall pass receivers, people who can kick, people who can pass and people who can receive, and return a kick-off as well as some to serve as captain and call plays. While it would be nice to get all of that in one person, it's neither likely nor practical.

Some Authentic Units

The best examples of implementing extra-curricular components and developing esprit de corps in my own classrooms occurred when I introduced authentic situations. When we transformed my seventh grade classroom into a "Westward Movement Museum" complete with model Conestoga wagons, audio tape instructions on building a sod house, the Oregon Trail drawn on the floor, girls in pioneer bonnets, news releases, ads, posters, pictures, drawings, diaries, a resource library, and stories of pioneer life, we had nearly every one of the characteristics listed above. We also had visits from other schools and a reporter from the *St. Louis Post Dispatch*.

Students in my high school journalism classes produced the school newspaper, yearbook, and creative writing journal, that were real products worthy of real feedback, operating on real deadlines, paid for by real subscription money, and providing real feelings of accomplishment, even earning real accolades.

Science projects for the county science fair; art projects for display at the state teacher's convention; civic club essay contests, citywide clean-up campaigns, tutoring in lower grades at the elementary schools, interviewing city officials, tape recording senior citizens for information on schooling in the good old days, the 7-11 store manager as a class speaker, veterans from three different wars on Veterans Day, a geometry class presentation to the school board, a school-wide anti-bullying campaign, and the spring music concert, are all authentic projects that can be an integral part of class subject content.

Offhand, I suspect that if the Algebra II class had to go on the floor of the gym as the basketball team does on a Friday night, in front of other students, classes, parents, community members, and the media, in "bowl" competition with Algebra II students from the rival high school, the activities during that preceding week would probably have been different. And if the rules called for full participation, not just the top students, there would no doubt have been some peer tutoring and cooperative learning preceding the event. Public performance is an incredibly powerful motivator.

Classrooms Should Be "Teams"

Often in classrooms, the teacher tries to be a coach, a leader, a referee, a facilitator, and a resource; but there is one big problem—he has no team. The class is too often a bunch of independent players all competing for the same position—top student or A student. Except for their being in the same room and all having similar individual achievement goals, the students are a conglomerate not a cohesive group. Each is concerned with his/her own progress and has no interest in the progress of others. It is only when a teacher can create a learning community wherein the students see that the way to reach individual goals is to work together sharing efforts, ideas while cooperating and helping one another as the best means of helping themselves.

Students learn from the company they keep; they strive to be like their friends; they value the things that those to whom the feel kinship value. Learning thus becomes more a matter of socialization and incidental learning rather than of instruction. Extra-curricular activities are dependent on learning through socializing and reciprocating in sharing mutual interests and goals. Teachers would do well to utilize cooperative relationship elements in the learning activities of the regular classroom.

Toward Greater Authenticity

Whenever teachers offer real authentic activities or lessons, they get real, authentic reactions with real authentic learning. When teachers build cooperative classroom communities, wherein each member from the least of them to the highest, share common goals and work together for their mutual benefit they become resources rather than taskmasters. Teachers can be resourceful, helping each kid rather than trying to reach each student through group lessons and class instruction. And, students can find and utilize many resources for learning in addition to the teacher.

While there are certainly other characteristics and other dynamics of extra-curricular activities, the obvious continued success of most of the programs, their popularity and voluntary participation, make them worthy of study, comparison, and emulation. The enthusiasm of the participants, the lack of extrinsic reward or at least its relatively minor role, the support, interest, and enthusiasm of those not directly participating or holding a leading role, and the long-lasting, continued interest in the activities are sufficient to use them as a model toward which teachers might aspire in academics as well as special subjects.

Fla. Tries to Avoid Flunking 50,000 Third Graders

The above headline, by Staff Writer, Marilyn Brown, appeared in the *Tampa Tribune* February 5, 2003. Fifty-thousand students had flunked the third-grade reading test. I read the article and wept. Through my anger, disgust and tears and with little thought, except for the potential devastation to the individual lives and families of thousands of innocent, victimized eight- and nine-year-olds, I wrote the following emotional reactions.

Since I reacted to Florida's decision to retain thousands of third graders, I have seen reports on sad, disastrous failure statistics from other states, including Texas, Iowa, North Carolina, and New York City. I am confident that every state has a similar story. How many lives shall we ruin?

186

Thoughts on Flunking 1000s of 3rd Graders

*Thousands of third graders can't all be rotten—maybe it is the hot Florida sun, the ocean breeze, or a virus brought in by snowbirds.

*If repeating the third grade doesn't teach them to read, repeating it a second and third time certainly will.

*I think the hardest problem with retaining third graders is going to be redefining "left behind" in the No Child Left Behind Act.

*Once we get them through third grade a second time, fourth-grade will be easy for them, right?

*And, don't worry about their attitude and about stigmatizing them—their former classmates, a grade ahead, will, of course, help them, as well as learn a lesson themselves, about the plight of the losers left behind and the value of their own success.

*Why not change the concept of what third grade is? Or what a third grader is? Or what grade level means? Or what should be taught? Or how it should be taught?

*What's with the time limit on learning to read? They didn't have a deadline for learning to walk, talk, or being potty trained, did they?

*Why not place a moratorium on any third grade curricula for the next year except reading and writing?

* Why not make reading inviting instead of pressurized grill, drill, and kill or teaching to the test, or teaching isolated skills?

* It's a good thing a lot of kids failed the test; if they had all passed, it would have shown the test was too easy and the "Standardistos" would have had to "raise the bar."

*Would you care to predict how many of the same kids will flunk again next year, and next, and next?

187

*Will there be about the same number of new failures in the next third grade classes? Maybe they can start a club.

*Shall we now worry about policy for kids over 18 years old still in third grade, or shall we wait to cross that bridge?

*Do we know what their status was as they entered third grade—they were probably all at the same level, right?

*Care to guess how many of the thousands were also retained at a previous grade level?

*Care to speculate whether any of the group were "children of color" "children of immigrants" or on subsidized lunch?

*Care to guess how many of them have been in trouble for their behavior or soon will be causing more trouble and having additional problems.

*Funny thing I didn't hear any blame attributed to the school system's failure—doesn't the system determine the five w's and an h? Come to think of it; what is the system's responsibility—to keep count of the failures? Good job!

*Doesn't the school district determine, initiate, and supervise the reading program, requirements, and procedures. Maybe we are flunking the wrong people?

*What if we moved the third grade test up a year and gave it at the end of fourth grade; I'd bet there would be a significant improvement without changing anything else.

*An extra year of school retention at $7,500 per pupil would be $3,750,000. Maybe they should "write-off" this year's failures and use that money to hire help for next year's third graders.

*Have the districts learned what to do so that this will be the last time for such failure? Maybe we should move the kids on until we learn the answer. No use having them repeat the grade until we do.

*Here's an idea: take the money that will be used to retest the kids, use it for re-teaching them and just assume they all passed rather than spend money testing them again.

*To insure non-discrimination let's fail a proportional number of school board member's, politician's, and administrator's kids too.

*Retaining them could be a good thing. Some parents have been known to deliberately hold their kids back so they will be older and more mature when they go out for football or volleyball and such.

*Let's lower the dropout age level so we can get rid of them rather than attempt to re-teach them.

*Let's promote them to 12th grade, give them a conditional diploma and declare them educated—end of failure problem.

*Applications now being accepted for third grade teachers in Florida.

* I think they should give a big bonus to the testing company for preventing these failing kids from slipping through third grade and lowering the fourth grade standards.

* Uh oh, better print up some more voucher forms and deposit more money in the transfer account.

*Maybe we aren't spending enough on their education. Andover, where President Bush went to school, charges $24,500 per year tuition.

*I'll bet some of the many "retirees" in Florida could be persuaded to participate in an "adopt a failing third grader" program.

*Let 'em flunk! Florida has plenty of use for tomato pickers, and workers to clean up after the tourists.

*Why aggravate the kids the rest of this school year? If they flunk the test, flunk them now for the year and avoid the June rush.

*Since they don't permit "social promotions," let's try "unsocial promotions."

*Check with the pharmaceutical companies, surely they have a pill for third grade failures—or at least they will develop one for that many customers—for a premium price.

*Let's beat them all. Everyone knows there's nothing a "good whooping" won't cure. Let's include the teachers and principals in the whoopings— get every one shaped-up. Maybe the Feds will pay for a whipping post and a cat of nine-tails.

*We could use a rack and thumbscrews or we could keelhaul them if the Feds will provide the materials and the keel. That's the problem, lack of materials to do the job.

*Take the money used for testing, tutoring, re-teaching and remediation, invest it for these students right now. By the time the third graders are 18, with wise investing, they can be rich enough not need reading and employment skills.

*If thousands of General Motor's cars in Florida ran off in the ditch in one year, it would be because of "bad drivers" not the fault of the cars, right?

*Third graders are certainly old and mature enough to suffer the consequences of their deplorable actions. I have no doubt they will see the wickedness of their ways, profit from the failing experience, redeem themselves, and thank the leaders for such devotion to excellence and tough love measures.

* How about double promoting them; they would have fifth graders as models, inspiration and help; and they would study extra hard not to have to go back to fourth grade—much less go back to repeat third grade.

*My own experience as a veteran teacher is that whatever might possibly be gained in knowledge by repeating the grade (zero to ten percent increase is the commonly expected gain) is offset by the attitude kids nearly always acquire as failures.

*I'm sure these nine-year-olds were okay when they came into the world. Whatever has happened to them since is not their fault—until now, of course.

*If only two had failed statewide, it would have been sad; but, since thousands failed it becomes an important historic statistic. Let's just keep score and report trends and statistical progress.

*Each child is living the only life she has; the only life she will ever have, the least we could do is not demean it or diminish it by declaring her a failure.

*These kids were not failures when they started kindergarten. Certainly they were not "labeled" failures. What happened? Is it something they did or they failed to do.

*You don't need research to determine what will most likely happen to these kids. Just remember in your own schooling those kids who were "failures," retainees or over-age at any grade level.

*If they would have checked on their pre-school lives, the school people could probably have predicted pre-natally that these kids would be ones who would fail.

*Would it surprise anyone to learn that the bottom ten percent of the first-grade class will remain the bottom ten percent throughout elementary school? What is it schooling does for them?

*Is there any reason to believe retention is worthwhile? That it is the best solution? That it is the only solution to the problem?

*At what point will Florida finally achieve the Lake Woebegone effect and thus solve the failure problem?

*I wonder how many of the third grader's parents were unsuccessful when they were in school?

*Here's an economical way to determine failures. Test just one class, take the failing kids, put them in another class; they will immediately attract the failing kids in that class and become good friends. Take those failing kids let them find the failures in other classes.

*Did anyone think of actually discussing it with the kids; not asking a couple of questions, actually engaging them in an extended discussion regarding their feelings and perceptions?

*Why not use the "open enrollment concept" where all third graders choose to go to fourth and then at any point in the year that they prefer to "go back" to third, they can.

*What are the chances that the families of these failing students will speak-up on their child's behalf or join an activist or support group. Shall we expect that these parents will become verbal, vocal, and politically astute in defense of their child's education?

*Shall we celebrate out leaders' commitment to tough love, to their own suffering, and pride at the equally tough decision that will surely solve the reading problem.

*Can you spell professional malpractice. Can you say legal action?

* How about this: anyone, other than teachers, directly involved in the decision to fail these third graders, must spend at least a week full time in any third-grade classroom, do a home visit, interview parents, and follow-up with a discussion with the kid after two months in the repeating process and a follow-up interview with parents.

If You Ask the Wrong Questions, You Get the Wrong Answers

The question, "What is the best textbook to use in this course?" might result in an excellent choice of textbook. But, the question, "Should we use a textbook in this course?" could result in an entirely different answer. With that prompt, one might consider using community resources, guest speakers, or multimedia sources in lieu of a textbook. However, the question, "Should we offer this course?" requires a very different set of considerations and different decisions. The question most frequently frames the answer, limits the alternatives, and always influences the answer.

For questions that are especially difficult to answer, maybe the question should be questioned before the answer is answered. Tough, nagging, chronic questions are probably so because of the complexity or ambiguity of the question, not because of difficulty in answering. To answer the question, "What should we do about the dropout problem?" other questions must first considered, "Who is the "we?" Society? The State? The school district? The school? The dropout's family? Is "problem" singular or plural? Does the "do about" refer to eliminating the problem, finding causes, or seeking alternatives? Are "dropouts" all in a single category or all subject to the same singular solution?

Every question has a set of assumptions and built-in limitations that are likely to determine or skew the answer. Word connotation, whom you ask, how you ask it, completeness of the answer and even, who's asking, context, and voice inflection, will help determine the answer. Political pollsters understand the question/answer relationship and use it to their advantage. I'm afraid too many educators argue about solutions without questioning their assumptions and considering the limited framework and undefined terms involved.

I wrote an article entitled, "We Get What We get" which appears as a part of this book. The article ends with this paragraph:

> Within the politics, mandates, mission, goals, strategic planning, curriculum, and educational policies, we take kids where they are and we teach them. We teach them whatever is required by those rules and within that structure. We Teach unconditionally—no excuses, no exceptions!"

A teacher named Laurie responded to the article by way of e-mail with the following concerns and question:

> So, how do we teach the kid who has had 5 hours of sleep, sees no value in the lessons we teach, watches his/her brother make hundreds of dollars selling drugs, does not even know how to spell his/her name correctly at age 10, and is sitting in our classroom day after day wondering what this school thing is all about? Not to mention, making it almost impossible to teach those students who do want to be there?
>
> After twenty years, I have also realized we are not going to change the kids we have right now, but how are we going to change this society to value education? Give me your tired, your poor...but how can we show them there is a way out of their situation? Maybe they are not college bound, but they also don't have to be on the path to the penitentiary.
>
> Answers? Laurie

I reply with the following:

> Dear Laurie:
>
> Thanks for your response to my article. I know that you are sincere in your reply, and I am pleased to respond with like candor:
>
> "So, how do we.......?" Who is the "we" of whom you speak. In my article I thought it was clear that the "we" is individual

teachers. In so many of the problems to which you refer, the "we" has to do with society, legislators, government, parents and administrators—people over whom I have no control and, so far as I can determine, little or no influence, whatsoever.

So answer #1 is: The most I as a teacher can do, is what I can do. I certainly cannot be expected to do more than I can do. But, the least I can do is what I can do. I will do what is within my purview, my jurisdiction, my decision making power; however limited. Somehow, I really do believe it is better to "light one little candle than to curse the darkness."

"...has had 5 hours sleep,..." If a kid has not had sufficient sleep, I would, after a discussion, consideration of alternatives and mutual decision, probably let him/her sleep in my class and try not to disturb him/her. S/He probably needs sleep more than s/he does my lessons and I would hope an administrator sees the kid sleeping and says something about it so I could explain my actions and maybe get some needed help.

"..does not even know how to spell his/her name correctly at age 10,.." If s/he can't spell his/her name after three years in school, I would begin with that issue as his/her individual curriculum rather than the third grade spelling list or other obviously inappropriate grade-three material designated for the class.

If he/she "sits there day after day" disengaged, I would give him/her some recognition or prestige; have him/her become my personal teaching assistant; show the other kids my respect for him; give her some responsibility; make him/her feel useful, or give him/her some special projects to do; solicit help from other adults to interact. In any case, I can guarantee you I would not let him/her "sit there doing nothing," even for a matter of minutes much less "day after day."

"...we are not going to change the kids we have now,..." WRONG! These are the kids we must change—it is where we have to start—today. What the nincompoops who framed the "No Child Left Untested Act" failed to understand is that the student achievement they demand will occur or fail to occur in the classrooms and it will happen to each student and involve each teacher in each classroom. We cannot neglect the students we have right now. Their time, as well as our time to act, is now.

Teachers do not need the lockstep, predetermined curriculum; the predigested, direct instruction, boring senseless lessons; the bureaucratic intrusion into classrooms; and they certainly don't need the meaningless, inappropriate, demeaning evaluation and ranking of their student's and their school's test scores. But teachers still have the opportunity each day to begin making changes within their limited realm of decision-making, if they will. They can create "wiggle room" within the school policies and they can find a degree of autonomy behind "their closed-door corner of their little world."

"...but, how are we going to change this society to value education?" While the answer lies, again, in the meaning of the word "we" and the definition of "society", education is the way it is because those in charge made it that way, and only they can

197

change it. Until those pompous, self-aggrandizing, non-educator, politico's come to the realization that teachers are the answer, not the problem, teachers must accept their relegated role and work within it. "Ya gotta dance with them that brung ya."

Teachers do the work of education and they must be empowered to determine the learning needs in their individual classrooms. They must have the autonomy to teach each child. Teachers are the heart and soul of education and they know their students better than anyone "up there" can possibly know individual students' needs. There is a difference in "knowing about" a kid and "knowing" a kid. I know my kids! Only their parents and immediate families could know them better. But even they do not know them as well as teachers in relation to schoolwork, school contexts and the teaching-learning process..

Meanwhile, unless or until the ninnies "up there" get their heads out of their arrogant, naive, deleterious, politically-motivated assessments, we, the teachers, must fight on behalf of the kids as well as ourselves, our profession and the parents. We, the individual classroom teachers, must begin the change process— changing our classroom procedures, our expectations, our attitudes, interactions and our daily activities.

We must reexamine our fundamental teaching-learning relationships and reflect on our individual responsibility for making a difference in our classrooms and ourselves each day, beginning right now. Neither we, nor our kids, have time to wait. I am the only one who can change me and you are the only one who can change you and how you choose to interact in your classroom. And, principals must work within their realm, superintendents and state department people must do what they can do and so on.

With Joy in Sharing,

Bill Page

Laurie's further response:

Dear Bill:

Thank you for your reply. Sometimes I feel like I am living on another planet and that my thinking about education is so off the mark. Thanks for making me feel a little better about swimming upstream. After 20 years, you'd think I would have become a little more calloused to the whole bureaucracy deal. Guess I have to realize that my love and caring is what kids need. I do know my kids and I thank you for all your comments. I will read your other articles, maybe during the Martin Luther King holiday. There is hope...I know. Thanks for reinforcing my thoughts. Laurie

Your comments and reactions to this article are welcome, billpage@bellsouth.net

Kids Are Always Learning

In any classroom, at any level, in any subject, with any type of kid, in any school, I can be certain that there will be at least seven categories of learning occurring continuously, simultaneously. While the intensity and level of awareness is constantly changing as the categories simultaneously vie with each other for attention, they are nevertheless a continuous part of every kid's learning experiences. All of them apply to every kid and to the teacher—their influence is never zero. The seven categories are these:

1. Relationships
2. Race, culture, class, physical (outward appearances)
3. Values
4. Teaching-learning interaction
5. Safety concerns
6. Physical environment
7. Hoping and thinking (despairing, dreaming, worrying, reflecting, wondering—"No mind is ever blank.")

Within the classroom, I know that these seven learning experiences are occurring continuously, every minute of every day. Each of us is constantly encountering experiences in each of these seven categories simultaneously. We cannot do otherwise. As kids come to class, their presence, regardless of planned teaching activities, will insure learning experiences. Following is a description of the experiences with examples to show what learning might be going on while teaching the planned lesson is occurring.

1. Relationships are there because the kids are there. They cannot help responding to fellow students that they like, dislike, greet, ignore, notice, speak to, are glad to see, observe working, talking, or interacting. All of this is enhanced or constrained by the class rules, policies, and procedures.

Examples: Two kids pass personal notes, get into a shoving match or exchange glances. Their relations are influencing their experiences.

2. Race, culture, class, and physical appearance are a part of each of us, whether we like it or not, regardless of whether it is good or bad. These elements are an integral part of us. They make us what we are, many or most of their characteristics and manifestations are omni-present. Anyone with whom we are in a relationship will be noticing, responding, and dealing with them at some level and to some degree, always.

Example: Comments about wearing old dirty clothes, or being called a "hillbilly" are made loudly enough to be overheard by the subject of the remarks. Even without the remarks, the "looks" are seen and understood.

201

3. Values "R" Us. Our behavior, especially including, attitude, non-verbal expression, subtle inferences, preferences, are our values. Whether we express our values deliberately or unconsciously, even deceitfully, they are there and they are a part of every thing we bring to a relationship and to a classroom.

Examples: "Math is stupid!" or "Sure, I hit him—my dad said I don't have to take anything from anybody."

4. Teaching-learning IS a relationship. Teaching-learning is what is occurring in any interaction because each member of the relationship is experiencing the other person. Those experiences cause us to reflect or react (including to ignore) or to respond internally or externally. The experiences range from some degree of thinking about it, or "rolling of the eyes" to enthusiastic support. What we learn is what we experience, including me experiencing you and vice versa—simultaneously. This is always occurring regardless of the traditional teaching and/or learning that might be happening.

Examples: One kid is showing another how to fold a paper airplane. A kid tells a dirty joke to another, who now may have "learned" several facts in a single exchange.

5. Safety is always conscious in everyone's mind. From basic survival concerns (if they are threatened) and emotional threats to constant physical dangers and potential harm. Everyone is continuously aware of the personal dangers of tripping, getting hit, or choking. In the

classroom where people are in immediate proximity there is bound to be a conscious or perhaps subconscious concern for a pencil jab, or punch being thrown, for bumping into one another, or to being made to feel stupid.

Example: Kids are playing, "Pass it on" and they surreptitiously hit every one on the shoulder or step on toes as they pass it. Punching or throwing an item, whether intending to be playful or not.

6. Classrooms are a place and, like any place, have its physical environment. Whether I am hot, or the room is hot or cold or noisy, whether there is sufficient light for me to read, whether people keep bumping into me, whether there is a comfortable place to sit and work, or whether I keep getting disturbed is an obvious part of the physical considerations for the environment. Allowing for all of the possible room conditions, coupled with people creating conditions, plus my own personal needs or situation such as the sun in my eyes, or my seat too near the door where my friends in the hall signal me, all make the environment quite important, influencing, and compelling.

Example: The humming of the fluorescent lights are disturbing the concentration of some kids, others don't notice it. Smells and sounds are occurring at some level all the time.

7. Hoping-Thinking. Our mind is always "working." Despairing, dreaming, wondering are integral, changing parts of our lives, whatever else we are doing. While we work or goof-off we are also

thinking about lunch, what happened last night or who we are and where we're going. Obviously, many factors from extremely personal, to the group functioning, to profound concerns about our self-worth and our future, contribute to what is going on in our minds besides what is intended or assumed by an outsider.

Example: A kid is worried about a bully who said, "I'll get you on the bus after school." He's mulling over what to do. He's having a conversation with himself and he was just called on by the teacher to answer a question.

Many teachers seem to be intuitively aware and interested in some of these intrusive and unobtrusive elements pervading students' minds during class time and teaching-learning objective and efforts. Some teachers seem to be unaware that a kid can be expected to ignore their parents getting a divorce, and memorize the poem. While teachers cannot possibly deal with each individual's attention to the seven competing attention-diverting conditions, they can reduce the frequency, severity, or intensity of the distractions and make some allowance for inward and outward detractors. Here are some suggestions:

- Putting the elements at a conscious level and considering their impact more frequently. Example: Having more empathy or consideration for the complexity and differences of individuals.
- Considering and reducing the possibility that kids may be being picked on for their individual differences.
- Modeling their own behavior and comments to specifically target the undesirable aspects of poor relationships, cultural differences, and values.

- Being more tolerant of what else might be going on in a kids head, and permitting more latitude in assignments, rules, and behavior expectations.
- Giving kids a greater opportunity to have input and participation in the decisions that affect their lives.
- Allowing a little more time for student responses and compliance.
- Allowing and offering choices in assignments whenever possible.

Remember: Each kid is living the only life he has; The only life he will ever have. We cannot change their parents, their home life, their experiences, or anything that has happened in their past, but, we can change what we are doing. The least we can do is not contribute to their problems and not participate in demeaning them.

Any way we can (1) improve their relationships with us and their peers, (2) reduce the discrimination possibilities, (3) allow for widely differing values, (4) improve the dynamics of our teaching, (5) provide a safe place to be at all times, (6) ensure good physical arrangement with changes and exceptions, and (7) encourage hope while reducing anxiety, would be a great starting place. Answer this question on behalf of any given kid in your class:

How would you like to have you for a teacher?

Teacher Self-Reflection

"I am the only one who can change me."

All teachers spend time assessing the job they are doing—they can't help themselves. Much of the time it is spontaneous or automatic and may or may not be useful. We see students react and we examine what we did or need to do. We see test or assignment results and we think about how we are doing. We plan or review tomorrow's lesson and we consider our goals. We work with a confused student and we evaluate or analyze his or her needs. We make out an assignment, test, or homework and ask about how it meets our goals. There is no doubt that teachers as professionals use self-evaluation and self-critique to help them do a good job. What might help them improve and learn to deal better with the at-risk kids is to use self-reflection as a more systematic, effective, and objective method of evaluation or assessment.

Self-reflection is like looking at a kind of mirror image of ourselves. It involves gathering information about ourselves and focusing on seeing our teaching behavior as others see it. Self-reflection requires critique—looking at both the positive and negative aspects. It requires systematic, ongoing and repeated assessment. (It also requires as much objectivity as possible, including videotaping, student feedback, friend and colleague observation, and authoritative questioning.) Most of all, self-reflection requires a specific, clear, behavioral set of goals chosen by the teacher. The teacher requests help from peers and instructional leaders and others of his or her choosing. The teacher decides what he or she wants them to observe and determines details of the observation and feedback processes.

For many teachers, the observations will include substitute teachers to permit peer observation. Self-reflection, for the purpose of improving a teachers ability to improve the achievement, is a process with as many facets and as much breadth and depth as we choose.

Following are examples of self-reflection that I have used in several situations in my career.

During my first year teaching, I let a tape recorder run during 5 periods of the eighth grade English classes I was teaching. My intent was to critique myself. It didn't help because I couldn't stand to listen to the stammers, stutters and repetitious words and phrases. Hearing my own voice in real-time, gave me an objective perspective of what my students were enduring. The fact that I couldn't stand it was powerful feedback that caused me to change. And, by the way, I let the kids know of my concerns about my teaching and my desire to improve. I asked their tolerance, help, and feedback.

Six years into my teaching, my "innovative, open" junior high installed TV cameras in several rooms. The cameras covered the entire room, were remotely controlled, and needed no operator. We as individual teachers could take our classes on chosen days to have our lesson recorded. We took the tape, watched it ourselves, and shared it, if we chose, with whomever we chose, for any purpose we chose. We could also erase it with no one having seen it. I used it several times, focusing on different dimensions each time.

As a member of a cross discipline team of four teachers (English, Social Studies, Math, and Science), I met daily with my seventh grade teacher team. As a Social Studies teacher, I met with the Social Studies department once a week; but, in an effort to personalize my individual performance, I chose two of the Social Studies teachers to observe me. I told them my concerns, objectives, and asked them to observe specific aspects of my teaching and asked them to react, to share their observations, and discuss the lesson. In several cases we involved the principal, assistant principal, and teachers from other subjects to observe and offer comments, suggestions, and ideas.

Many changes in my teaching are specifically documented, and I have made some dramatic changes in my teaching (e.g., my questioning technique) as a result of these and other self-reflection incidents. Teachers get their feedback and satisfaction from their student's reactions and progress. However, they are not likely to get much honest feedback from the students at-risk unless they make a special effort. By learning to respond to the feedback and their own needs and concerns, teachers can improve the teaching-learning process and use their peers and on going reflection to improve their teaching and their ability to close the achievement gap.

There are many books and many journal articles devoted exclusively to teacher self-reflection. Many of the books recommend specific, structured procedures and have numerous suggestions for their use.

Self-reflection as crucial to improving instruction, and I recommend at least scanning some of these resources and devising a personal approach. In any case, each teacher must take and keep control of the process in its entirety. An essential in the effectiveness of this procedure is the belief that learning things about yourself, however disconcerting or even painful, should result in procedures for improvement.

Imposed Authority vs. Natural Authority

OR

How to Get Kids to Sit Down, Shut Up, Pay Attention, Follow Directions, and Want to Learn

Master Sergeant Mitchell, Company "D" Drill Sergeant, explained in clear, unmistakable terms: "I can't make ya do nothin', but I can make ya wish ya hadda done it." I was not a "good soldier." I was drafted into military service, I did not volunteer, my claw marks are still on the kitchen floor where the draft board dragged me out, kicking and screaming. Sgt. Mitchell had authority over me. It was probably absolute authority; I don't know because I never had the nerve to check out any rights I might possibly have had. But, I do know it was imposed authority. And surely enough, he was right. I found he could make me very sorry if I did not do whatever he ordered. So, just as surely, I did everything he ordered.

Lesson One

The punishment/reward system of imposed rules and requirements was alive and well in "Dog" company. I didn't like KP duty, forced marches, push-ups, close-order drill, or scrubbing barracks floors with a toothbrush. On the other hand, I did like weekend passes, PX privileges, ball games, and movies. I learned my lessons well. I did what I was told, the way I was told, when I was told, because I was told. When necessary, the drill sergeant reinforced the imposition with a reminder, "Youse meatheads play ball wit me, I play ball wit you. Youse don't play ball; I shove da bat down yer troat." (Or words to that effect.) His discipline strategies worked. I became a soldier, not a good one nor a bad one, just an acceptable one, for one year, eleven months and eighteen days. Then I got my discharge papers and I never again did anything the sergeant "taught" me.

Lesson Two

Back in the days when Don Faurot was coach at Missouri University—not merely the stadium and the parkway now named after him. Faurot and his coaching staff had unquestioned authority over me in all matters pertaining to my football career—everything from my weight, to my summer job, my off-season conditioning, my academic progress, my "grant-in-aid," and in practice and games. Coach Faurot did not use rewards or punishment. Neither did he use coercion, intimidation, threats, or anxiety. He had natural authority. I did everything he asked not because Coach could make me do it or even "make me wish I had" but because I voluntarily chose to do his will.

If the goal is to win football games, and Coach Faurot knows what that takes and how to go about it, then, I was very anxious to do whatever he asked promptly, with willing cooperation, and with a high degree of enthusiasm and commitment. I found satisfaction in calisthenics, wind sprints, tackling dummies, blocking sleds, and extra drills. You certainly couldn't call it fun. We called it hustle, esprit de corps, or morale. I willingly relinquished my authority to the coach.

Lesson Three

Good teachers have natural authority in their classrooms. They know what students need to know and need to do to be successful or to master the subject. Teachers know what is necessary to pass tests, score well on the SATs, get good report cards, increase grade point averages, or succeed in the next grade or in college. Teachers know the course requirements, prerequisites, and expectations. They know what constitutes course proficiency and what skills and study procedures are important. Such teachers have natural authority, and their students usually respond well and have a good attitude; and maybe even hustle, esprit de corps, and morale.

Since teachers know what it takes to learn the course content, students are willing to relinquish their own authority, willing to do whatever they are told, and often more than they are told, without being told. However, there always seems to be some " reluctant learners," "trouble-makers," "bad kids" who can't or won't cooperate. Who don't or won't sit down, shut up, pay attention, follow instructions, or want to learn. They are notorious, we have all gone to school with them, had them in our classes, kicked them out of our classes, spent hours of precious time on them, and have been frustrated by their disrupting our lessons, our classes, and their interfering with the other kids learning.

Uncooperative Students

These uncooperative students create one of three problems that preclude the use and effectiveness of natural authority. First, they don't know they need what is being taught; second, they don't want to know what is being taught; third, they can't comprehend what is being taught. Each of these problems requires a different approach by the teacher. Students who don't know they need the course need to be shown its value. This is done through a student-teacher relationship of mutual respect. If I don't like you or "your type;" if I don't think you understand me; or if I don't think I can be like you; I will not listen to you. On the other hand, if I trust you, respect you, or think you have my interest at heart, then I will listen and can be shown reasons to learn.

Unacceptable Choices

Students who don't want to know what is being taught must be given a viable reason, an acceptable reason or, at least, an alternative. Many of us, when we were students, reasoned that a particular course was of no value in itself but would help us toward our degree. So we tolerated it, forgot it, and moved on. Students with long range goals such as pleasing people, passing or getting credit, making good grades, or graduating can use the same reasoning we did. Those who do not have such goals must be offered viable alternatives. They already have alternatives, but skipping, disrupting, entertaining themselves, amusing others, and various unacceptable ways of relieving their boredom are neither good nor acceptable choices.

Teachers Must Offer Alternatives

Those students who can't understand what is being taught, who do not have the prerequisite knowledge, are confused, or who lack study skills, cannot be expected to sit down, pay attention, or behave, at least not hour after hour, day after day, month after month, year after year. They can fake it, respond to coercion, or tolerate meaningless activity for only so long. Teachers must insure that students have the prerequisites and must eliminate student confusion.

Imposing Authority is Mis-Education

There are books and courses on relationships; there are ways of making courses relevant through integrated lessons and authentic learning; and there are more remediation approaches than there are students who need remediation. All have the potential to eliminate the hassle with reluctant learners by using natural authority. To continue imposing our authority through coercion, compulsion, intimidation, bribery, rewards, and punishment, constitutes "mis-education."

We know that it is possible for teachers to get compliance through imposition of authority; but to get the commitment that results in meaningful, lasting learning, teachers must help their students choose to learn. If students learn something and later forget it, does that count or matter? What is the value of saying, "I used to know how to find square root, but I don't remember how to do it now."

Students Who Choose to Learn

In the matter of classroom control or discipline the question is, Do you want techniques such as Sgt. Mitchell used that can make a student sit down, shut up, pay attention, follow directions and want to learn? Or, do you want, as Coach Faurot used, a way to have a student choose to sit down, shut up, pay attention, follow directions and want to learn? Teachers who seek better ways to control behavior are very different from teachers who provide reasons for behavior—so are the students who choose to learn rather than who are made to learn, and so is the quality and duration of their learning. Teachers who use natural authority don't need to use imposed authority.

For a full description of the dicipline ideas in this article go to:

www.teacherteacher.com

or

E-Mail: billpage@bellsouth.net

Bill Page

and

Dr. Ed Frierson, past president of the International Association of Childeren with Learning Disabilities, present a two hour, two DVD discipline package,

Personal Style Discipline

Mandating vs. Teaching; People vs. Products

In the work-a-day world people generally have jobs dealing primarily with people or with products. Those in charge of products such as automobiles, Tee shirts, paper clips, canned goods, or widgets, may also have to deal with the people who work there. Their job is to control production conditions. To control the workers, as a means of controlling quality, production, and conditions, they can post rules about washing hands and wearing safety goggles, and they can make announcements, send memos, give warnings, and call them "on the carpet. Some employees of a manufacturing company may work exclusively with people. A personnel manager has hiring, firing, and welfare decisions.

Those who work with people such as judges, politicians, and state offices for employment, welfare, and parolees, doctors, prison guards and army sergeants, have objectives, laws, policies, requirements, standards, and procedures. It is easy for an "outsider" to complain about "letting guilty

217

people go free," or about releasing dangerous people from prisons. We are a nation of laws, policies, and regulations. The "outsiders" may not understand the laws, and some workers may "fudge" on the policies, but if the policies are not working of the staff is not doing its job we can change the policies and we can fire the staff.

Teachers are in the people business. Kids are not products; they are kids— human kids. We cannot treat them as inanimate objects, because they are not. We can apply laws, rules, and policies to them and to the institution. We can't treat them like workers in a plant or in an industry.

The difference in working with kids in school is that:

- You can't reject their application.
- You can't fire them for rule infractions.
- You can't reject them and request a better model.
- You can't expect a better crop next year.
- Kids can't select a "major" according to his/her interest.
- Kids can't change a course because they don't like math.
- Kids don't select their teachers, texts, schedules, evaluations.

Being a kid is only a temporary job—they will outgrow it: Teachers cannot fire them for failing to do quality work, for not meeting minimum standards, for failing to show up for work, for inattention, apathy, or attitude. In short, we are stuck with the kids in school, you can't bar or restrict their enrollment or attendance. You can't mandate their learning.

You can mandate their behavior, and with sufficient rewards and punishments you can get a high degree of compliance, but there is still a serious problem—controlling them is not teaching them. Contrary to what many teachers think, our goal is to teach kids to behave not make them behave. I know that there are those who think forcing them to make their beds teaches them to make their beds. Rather, they must learn the value of making the bed and learn to want to make the bed before they will willingly do it. It is our job as teachers to teach kids the value and importance of learning.

Just Ask the Kids

"There is one thing I know that no one else on earth knows—and that is how I feel about the things that impinge on my life. You may think you know. You may think you can interpret my mood, reactions, and feelings. You may think you can relate to my plight. But you will never know unless you ask—unless you get it from me. And, if you are nice, sincere, genuinely interested, and go about it in the right way; you might even get me to share that personal information with you."

What could be more important to our desire for more effective teaching and improved learning than finding out how the kids feel about what goes on in the classroom? No matter how much we know or think we know about our class(es) our subject(s), our kids, and the grade level we teach, we could probably learn more. I have had considerable success by having class discussions to give the kids a feel for some of the topics and feelings, and especially to show them my feelings and desires too.

How do your students feel about your class? About you? Your teaching? Assignments? Grades? Tests? Learning? The quality or quantity of their own learning? Their part?

Which teaching procedures do your students like best? Like least? What might they like to change? Do they have "pet peeves?" Find out what advice this year's class has for you and your new students for next year.

Which classroom rules would they like to see modified? Or added? Or eliminated?

What do your kids do outside of class? In other classes? In their favorite classes?

What about kids previous school experiences? Previous classes and teachers?

What are your kids proud of? What inspires them to work hard? What are some memorable experiences they have had in school? What do they think I should be sure to do again with next year's class(es)?

What are some things they would like me to know about them and their feelings? Are there some things I could do that would help them do better in my class?

Some Considerations

Have someone else lead a discussion or offer a survey or questionnaire...counselor, last year's teacher, a teacher they don't have for class, apprentice teacher, or college student. Exchange classes for a day or two to get feedback from the kids for the regular teacher.

Seek feedback in bits...after a lesson or after using a particular, or experimental technique, after a test, or a grading period, or with students in small groups.

Make plans for feedback and ask colleagues for suggestions and input.

Invite next year's teacher(s) to come in this year as a guest speaker. Get yourself invited to talk to the kids who might be assigned to you for the next year.

Have a committee of your kids talk to and answer questions for next year's potential students. Have some students from last year come in to tell this year's class what to expect.

Devise surveys, and specific reasons for surveys. Create a variety of feedback procedures.

An Afterword

Moments ago, I entered the three-word title, At-Risk Students into the Google Search Engine. Seventeen seconds later the computer showed 22,200,000 entries. Seems like a lot of other people have something to say about at-risk students. Thousands of educators, organizations, parents, professionals, and college professors have dedicated their lives, money, and time to researching at-risk needs and problems. I was a part of the phenomenal origin, growth, and development of the learning disabilities movement, which in the past half century, went from an idea to the involvement of 25 million kids, educators, and professionals. I saw the progression. I made session presentations at sixteen of the first seventeen national conferences. I keynoted a National Conference of the Canadian Association of Children and Adults with Learning Disabilities. The learning disabilities component is by far the largest category included in the at-risk label.

What should be done about the at-risk problems? Consider this task: Peruse the resource catalog of the Association of Supervision of Supervision and Curriculum Development—the answers are there. With thousands of books, videos, kits, seminars, programs, consultants, and monthly journal that goes to 175,000 educators, all phases of the problems are addressed, analyzed, defined, and resolved. Each book alone claims to have the answers or at least the approach. It says so on the back of the cover, in the preface, and in the contents. Collectively, these sources must surely have successful ways to teach the currently failing students. If not, dozens of other publishers, organizations, and individuals claim to have "the way." I have decided the at-risk problem is like dealing with body odor, bacteria-free toilets, losing weight, or credit card debt, all we need to do is follow the advice of authorities or television commercial writers and "Poof"—no more problem; except, of course, the problem of whether you have sought sufficient advice, which advice to accept, whether you follow the advice, and how to interpret, adapt, and implement it. The data are overwhelming and continue to "whelm." I am reminded of the old aphorism: If you know enough to distinguish good advice from bad advice; you don't need the advice.

What Does and Doesn't Work

Through my forty-six years as a teacher, education books and journals touted programs, reforms, techniques, and research. My colleagues and I struggled to teach all students including the students in school most at-at risk. With full class loads and with no help from the experts, we encountered the daunting problem of "more" and it easily defeated us—more poverty, more students at-risk, more flunking, more complaining, more drop-outs, more regulations. Of course the problem of "less" hit us hard too—less, time, less money, less respect, less tolerance, less help, less accommodation.

I began with a singular proposition; I don't know what works with these students, but I sure as heck know what doesn't work. There is a long record of failing strategies. What doesn't work is everything that has been done thus far. If the strategies worked, we would be succeeding wouldn't we? What doesn't work is flunking them, raising the bar, repeating the grade, punishing them, withholding privileges, dumbing-down their lessons, condescending attitude, pitying, testing, remediating, reinforcing, regrouping, and mollycoddling.

Six Years of Research On At-Risk Students

From "commonsense experiences" with this singular class of "the bottom" seventh graders, I submitted a program proposal, which led to my creating and directing a six-year research project funded by the U. S Office of Education and later by Peabody College and the Kennedy Child Study Center. Six years of research: three years with troublemakers in suburb schools of St. Louis and three years with inner-city troublemakers in Nashville was developed, implemented, replicated, and researched on two premises. First, student discomfiture is the schools' fault and the schools' problem, not the students; not the parents. Failure results from inappropriate curriculum and instruction. It is a mismatch between what is offered with what students need. Second, learning is a personal, private, individual experience that is the students' responsibility. No one can learn anything for students. It is they who need to be concerned and interested; it is they who need to do the thinking and planning; and it is they who need to exert the learning effort.

This concept of learning is diametrically opposed to what most teachers have experienced or been taught. Because the traditional system "worked" for teachers and others who were successful in school all the way through college, it is easy to think failure is the fault of the student rather than the system. Successful teachers too were responsible for their own learning, but they attributed their learning to the education system's responsibility, without their really understanding why. It is the old story of schools taking credit for successful students but blaming the unsuccessful students for their own failure. If the teacher plans and directs students' learning and it doesn't work, it is the teacher who has failed. If students are in charge of themselves and their learning choices, they choose what makes sense to them and avoid what doesn't. That alone will result in success.

The thirty-six teachers who worked with me, learning to shift the learning responsibility back to students, where it was originally and where it belonged. Each team of two teachers in eighteen schools in Missouri and Tennessee gave up their "good classes" to work with students most seriously at-risk, gave up their Summers for project workshops, battled school policies on grading and testing, and fought the condescending attitude of many other teachers and students. For their effort and devotion and successes, the program teachers received only the personal satisfaction of salvaging and transforming some kids' damaged lives. Recognition of the success of the program was limited to those directly involved and was never disseminated, although more government money was spent on that phase of the program than on the other parts all together.

A Highly Successful Research Program

A successful research project is like publishing a book; of 10,000 submitted only one is accepted. Of 50,000 accepted only one will make the "better" selling list, much less the "best" selling list, however obvious the success is to those involved. Project teachers, taught the concepts of acceptance, attitude, identity, and relationship, went their own way and I went mine. My way is described briefly in the Meet Bill Page section of this book.

What I personally learned about teaching all kids, but particularly about the needs of those at-risk, from those years of research and subsequent teaching experiences is that I am a teacher, no more, no less. (Conversely, there are a lot of "educational titles" that I am not.) As a classroom teacher, no one in authority ever asked me what I thought about, modular schedules, report cards, learning disabilities, special education, "mainstreaming," or the "No Child's Behind Left Act." [Rearranged title is mine.] Actually, I told them anyway without being asked, but it was a futile cry in the night. I make decisions for me in my class, in my school—period. That's it! Principals make decisions for their teachers in their school, in their district, and so it goes. We each make decisions within our authority realm; Superintendents make decisions within the realm or superintendents, not the realm of the State Departments of Education. However, within my own closed-door classroom kingdom the most valuable lesson I learned is this:

I Make The Decisions In My Classroom

I make the decisions in my classroom and no one has ever made one for me. I make my decisions on the basis of my contractual relations and my professional obligations. I make decisions according to my commitment to the district that pays me and to its mission. I make decisions within my responsibility to my students and my accountability to their parents. I make decisions with regard to the teacher next door and the teachers next year. I make my decisions within the rules, policies, and procedures of this school system and I make my decisions on the basis of my personal and professional life. But they are still my decisions.

Because of my decisions, the desks are faced this way instead of that, arranged in a circle or moved or turned at the desire of each student. The reason there are twenty questions on the test instead of ten; they are essay instead of true-false, they are timed and "spelling counts" or not timed and "spelling doesn't count." When you see students in my room sitting or lying on the floor with their shoes off, it is because of my decisions in relation to students' decisions.

For the record, in my classroom, the reason kids can take any test over again is because I permit it to be taken over again—and I don't average the grades. The reason we spend three days reviewing for a test, or take a practice test instead of taking a "pop quiz," is because it's my decision. I concluded that I could let a kid struggle with work he could not possibly do, or I could help him find something appropriate. I could give an "incomplete" instead of an F so that more time could be spent learning. I could involve the students in the decisions; or I could make all the decisions in advance and merely announce them. I could use encouragement rather than punishment. In short, I do what I do because it is my classroom, my choices and my responsibility. Students respond by their decisions interacting with mine. Not as a compromise, but through mutual decisions based on mutual understanding of the position of one another.

A Matter of Teacher Priority

So while all the forces exerted on me temper my decisions, I make my decisions within that constraint and I take full advantage of any "wiggle room" I can get. I push the limits of my authority as a teacher. And, if you make me choose between defying a rule and wiping out a struggling kid— you will probably find that I have "carelessly forgotten the rule," have "interpreted the rule differently from your expectation," or I am prepared to argue vehemently if you challenge me. You might also find me in your office, stomping the floor, pounding the desk, "in your face," and slamming my contract down like a gauntlet.

I wrote this "Afterword" even though I found the word has been omitted from the dictionary. (Must have been Mr. Webster's inadvertent oversight—it's a great word.) I feared that putting this information as a foreword might have caused some teachers to write me off as a "kook" or "wild-eyed liberal." But I figured that after teachers read at least some of my reasonable ideas, thoughts, and essays, they might see that I really do believe in advocating for defenseless and abused students.

A Pervasive, Persistent, Pernicious Problem

Through careful self-examination, critique, reflection, and analysis of my forty-six years of teaching kids and teachers, I am all the more convinced that the most pervasive, persistent classroom problem teachers encounter on a daily basis is the two or three and frequently even more students in each class, who are labeled at-risk and who exhibit a wide range of disruptive, aggravating, relentless interference with orderly teaching-learning processes.

A story making the rounds when I was a young teacher, went like this:

"What is the ideal class size?" is the question.

"Three fewer than I have now." is the answer, "If I can pick the three."

Teachers smile or laugh, knowingly, at the story, but it goes on.

"There will be another three take the place of the three just eliminated, and then another three, another three until it gets down to only two students left —and one of them is causing problems and failing to keep up with the other."

Disengaged Students Create Problems

These problem students are certainly the basis of the most verbal, vocal, complaints I hear from teachers. A look at the dozens of message boards, blogs, and chat rooms of web sites such as <http://www.teachers.net> where teachers have an opportunity and place to discuss, clearly shows the teacher frustration, complaints, negative comments, requests for help, and occasionally, desperation. Whether teachers blame kids or complain about parents, administrators, politicians, society, or television and electronic games and devices, no one should question the prevalence and severity of the at-risk problem. Under chat board titles of discipline, classroom management, beginning teachers, or various categories of student problem labeling, who could doubt that a few students in each class cause most of the problems?

Class Disruptions Are Disruptive

Classrooms are structured for group instruction and for the most part require a quiet, orderly, cooperative atmosphere. Most any deviation can distract and upset the planned procedures. A major disruption can wipe out the remainder of the period. One non-conforming student can redirect attention, cause lost instructional time, and divert the teacher's attention and action for a considerable amount of time. Unfortunately there seems to be little or no allowance for such disruptions or loss of time on task, or for teachers' attention to be focused on a single deviant child. Such a diversion leaves 20 plus students also focusing on the teacher-to-problem-child interaction, and a chance to divert, temporarily, their thinking to their own priorities.

Disengaged students are sure to cause difficulty at some level and to some degree in virtually every classroom, every day, year after year. They are first among the chronic failures who sap the teacher's time and energy, disrupt instructional procedures and require inordinate effort of administrators at all levels, school counselors, social workers, psychologists, truant officers, and other school personnel. When a student is not engaged in the class work, her attention is necessarily on "something else." That is a constant, continuing problem. Students, disengaged because they are unable to participate, are left sitting, doing nothing, looking for ways to entertain themselves and others. The cause of disengagement that needs to be addressed first, and should not be assumed to be a matter of student choice.

Recall "Problem Kids" of Our Youth

Most of us, if not all, went to school with problem students. The number of such students, the degree of deviation and the teachers' ability to control the extent of the class interference varied, but the students were in every class. Class misbehavior is probably more prevalent in our memory of our years in school than is the learning or any of the routine incidents. We are all sure to remember the problem students who were in our classes. It is easy to recall their classroom apathy, disrespect, and attention getting behaviors. We still remember their names and can describe the antics of the clowns, the troublemakers, and those who were over-age and over-size, who entertained the class and who were seemingly unafraid of authority figures and oblivious to ominous or even actual consequences. I remember hiding my delight and secretly cheering them on. It was kind of like rooting for the outlaws in a John Wayne Western.

Childhood Is Only Temporary

These "kids," we went to school with, are still with us. They are still in every classroom at every grade level still creating the same disruptions and causing the discipline problems handled the same way. We remember specific incidents, laugh about anecdotes, gossip, and joke about the bad kids—we even recall their names. Childhood is only a temporary condition; kids grow into adulthood whether or not they succeed in school or cause trouble and drop out. As older students move through the schools, new ones take their place. As adults, except for those who wind up in prison, they are mostly hidden from those of us who at least appear to be living a happy and successful adult life. In the world of work, the under-educated, under-employed and the functionally illiterate have increased through, greater poverty, technological job outsourcing, increased immigration, population growth, and more highly skilled jobs.

233

What is different now is that there are no longer havens, inconspicuous jobs, family farms, or remote locations for the students who failed in school, failed to get an education, dropped out, were expelled and who became a part of adult society—marginally, of course. Each day 300 students drop out of school. They "leave" when old enough, when there is nothing in school for them, when their misery is too great, or when they can stand the futility no longer.

What Teachers Can Do

The world has changed. Society's needs have changed. But schools and the educative process remain the same. Teachers are not responsible for the mandates and policies that create problems for students at-risk, and they cannot implement reforms on the students' behalves; but, teachers can make a difference in the teacher-student relationship by empathizing with the student's dilemma, understanding the causal factors, and recognizing the defensive measures used by at-risk students to hide their problems and their anguish. Imagine sitting through hour after hour, day after day without involvement or interest, worried that you might appear incompetent or stupid; and, thinking that it will never get any better, only worse. As a starting point, teachers can take responsibility for accepting responsibility to teach all students including those most at risk, and they can use their responsibility, decisions, and options to:

✓ Adjust their teaching methods,
✓ Apply proven, more current, techniques,
✓ Develop new procedures,

✓ Utilize differentiation strategies,
✓ Increase student responsibility for learning,
✓ Examine existing attitudes,
✓ Encourage more student participation,
✓ Critique their teaching-learning interaction,
✓ Give students more input and opportunity,
✓ Communicate more meaningfully with the parents
✓ Utilize new brain-mind research
✓ Review and renew educational priorities,
✓ Recommit to student-centered learning,
✓ Conduct class meetings and discussions.
✓ Utilize new technology,
✓ Use a team approach,
✓ Use pair sharing and study buddies
✓ Use multi-modality learning,
✓ Introduce authentic learning,
✓ Use production-driven activities,
✓ Create a community concept
✓ Use unit and project activities,
✓ Use hands-on activities,
✓ Use small group interaction.

Regardless of the mindless, bureaucratic nightmare within which teaching at-risk students occurs, the simple fact is this; students are compelled to come to our classes, they have no choice, and we are required to teach all who are assigned to us. We have no choice. There is no viable alternative on either side. Teachers have the obligation to change the teaching learning conditions. Our job is to teach all students, who are accepted by the school—no exceptions, no excuses.

I am pleased to end with what should have been the foreword in this book. Correctly, it should have been on the back of the front cover in spite of its unethical, irreverent flavor.

Here Is My Story
However ugly, it is the truth.

At age twenty-seven, with no interest whatsoever in teaching, I took a stopgap job as an eighth grade English teacher. I was totally unprepared to teach. I had no commitment and I had a lousy attitude, "If I don't like it I'll quit, whether that's at the end of the first day or first week." I didn't like kids. I didn't dislike them either–I just didn't know what they were or anything about them.

Somehow, by blundering through a day at a time, and sacrificing students learning and curriculum, I began to figure out enough of what was happening and why. With unwanted feedback, unsolicited help, and lots of useless advice from administrators, colleagues, and friends, who had totally different goals, I learned to teach. (I found that giving me advice was frequently helpful to the advice givers.) I was glad to be of assistance. Offering advice always seemed to make their day and it sometimes made me feel useful.

Now, after forty-six years, I am delighted to share my strategies for teaching-learning success. However unorthodox, iconoclastic, and unheralded my teaching techniques, they are all tested and proven— by me. In addition to learning survival skills that kept me from being fired--I learned crucial teaching skills not taught in teacher training. I learned that many of the great teachers owe their greatness to discovering unspoken, highly effective survival skills, including but not limited to the following:

I Learned All About:

- ✓ Out-bureaucrating the bureaucrats
- ✓ Covering my posterior
- ✓ Avoiding faculty gossips,
- ✓ Ignoring school memos
- ✓ Using student feedback
- ✓ Begging forgiveness,
- ✓ Never asking permission;

I acquired successful teaching strategies of:

- ✓ painful self-reflection,
- ✓ lots of trial-and-error,
- ✓ plagiarizing ideas
- ✓ adapting and adopting lessons
- ✓ ploys, plots and stratagems,
- ✓ more feedback than I ever wanted.

I exploited incidental and accidental lessons of:

- ✓ desperation and panic
- ✓ rationalization and defensiveness
- ✓ deliberate forgetfulness and avoidance
- ✓ naivety and ignorance.

I learned to be a successful, satisfied teacher of successful, satisfied students. And am pleased to share my success strategies with others. I will save sharing my failures for another book.

Note: I love to receive e-mail. As a writer, random, sporadic, and unexpected e-mail messages provide useful distractions and quite frequently some food for thought, argument, and provocative disagreement. I received a message from a retired superintendent who told me he had heard my presentations on a CD that told my refusing to give F's and refusal to grade or mark papers. He let me know that I should have been fired for unprofessional conduct, indicted for unethical behavior, and sued for malpractice--I love it!

If you have comments, questions, issues, or time to exchange ideas, I am usually home staring at my computer monitor, wondering why all of the profound thoughts I put into the keyboard come out like second-grade gibberish. I love to hear from people who care about kids and have a desire to protect them from the cruel school.

With joy in sharing, billpage@bellsouth.net.

Annotated References

These books have influenced my writing. Mostly they have influenced my life, my teaching, and my thinking tremendously. I recommend them to everyone seeking to separate the truths in education from the insidious myths and harmful traditions that impede the teaching-learning process. Their commonality lies in their impinging on my underlying thoughts and ideas involving classroom decision making, I have included some that represent my core beliefs and that came along at turning points in my teaching career, many of them in the early, formative stages of my dissatisfaction with the school system and my becoming an advocate for vulnerable students. There is a proverb that says, "When the student is ready, a teacher will come." I am pleased for you to meet some of my most effective "teachers."

Bracey, Gerald W., *The Death of Childhood and The Destruction of the Public Schools*, 2003, Heineman, Portsmouth NH. Bracey is the only writer I know with an unimpeachable record and credentials, who advocates for teachers, students and commonsense. His defense of the schools, indictment of its critics and impeccable research is the reason I regard his writing so highly (and *Phi Delta Kappan* runs his columns and Golden Apple Awards.).

Cantor, Nathanial, *The Dynamics of Learning*, 1946, Foster & Stewart Publishing, Buffalo, NY. A life-altering incident is one, "after which ones life will never be the same again." This book and Dr. Cantor simple statement, "You can lead a student to a classroom or a textbook, but you can't make him learn unless he wants to or wills to learn." marked the first life-altering incident in my teaching. It became my first meaningful struggle to reconcile the dichotomy between my expressed belief and my denial in practice.

Delisle, Robert, *How to Use Problem-Based Learning In the Classroom*, Association for Supervision and Curriculum Development, Alexandria, VA. The author gives simple explanations with plenty of examples in all subject areas. Teachers must learn "How to" and use the approach immediately.

Dexter, Lewis Anthony, *The Tyranny of Schooling*, 1964, Basic Books, New York / London. Professor Dexter devoted many years to the study of what special educators call, Educationally Mentally Retarded. He discovered, to his astonishment and indignation that these problems were often actually created and increased by the schools. He claims the school system fosters "stupidity" in "troubled" children.

England, Crystal M., *Uphill Both Ways; Helping Students Who Struggle In School*, 2004, Heinemann, Portsmouth, NH. The sensitivity England shows through plain talk and first hand experience, makes her a kindred spirit and this book with her three R's—Relationship, Relationship, Relationship a delight and a basic tool for teachers of students at-risk.

Franklin, Barry, (Ed) 1998, *When Children Don't Learn*, Teachers College Press, New York. "Failure to learn represents a virtual assault on the very act of teaching and on the work of those whose identities are subsumed in that role. Shame accompanies failure as well as the fear of failure that follows.

Perceiving, Behaving Becoming -Lessons Learned, Assn for Supervision / Curriculum Development. Alexandria, VA. For 30 years I have been proclaiming the 1962 ASCD yearbook, *Perceiving Behavior, Becoming* "The Best Book I Have Ever Read, a mind-blowing, life-changing revelation." In 1999 ASCD re revived the fabulous book and includes responsive updates and applications by contemporary educators such as Alfie Kohn. Originally, in 1962, the ASCD invited four authorities to write essays on what is necessary to develop "self-actualized" students. The four authors are: Earl C Kelly; Carl Rogers; Abe Maslow; and Arthur W Combs. For me that's enough said about the book.

Glasser, William, *Schools Without Failure*, 1969, Harper & Row, New York. Very few children come to school failures, none come labeled failures; *it is school, and school alone which pins the label of failure on children.* Most of them have a success identity, regardless of their homes or environments. In school they expect to achieve recognition and, with the faith of the young, they hope also to gain the love and respect of their teachers and classmates. The shattering of this optimistic outlook is the most serious problem of the elementary schools. Whatever their background, children come to school highly receptive to learning.

Glatthorn, Allen A., *Performance Standards & Authentic Learning*, 1999, Larchmont New York. Eye On Education. The

241

author defines most of "standards" terms in current writing, and distinguishes differences among the terms and labels. His emphasis is on learning rather than teaching and he gives a straight forward, useable application of authentic learning as an individual matter that has real life value and is constructed by the learner. Every thing else he offers is practical teacher application.

Gross, Ronald and Beatrice, *Radical School Reform*, 1969, Simon & Schuster, Inc, New York. The Grosses bring together the voices of 22 outstanding educators who were dissatisfied with the impact of schooling on children. Each author has written entire books on reforming education, giving an opportunity to sample the feelings and concerns of leading school reformers, including Holt, Kohl, Kozol, Neill, Leonard, Dennison, and Friedenberg.

Hargis, Charles H., *Grades and Grading Practices, Obstacles to Improving Education and to Helping At-Risk Students*, 1990, Charles C Thomas Publisher, Springfield IL. This book explores the problems caused by grades, calling attention to how present grading practices created obstacles to improving the quality of education by not helping students who are at-risk. Students at-risk are demoralized by poor grades, bringing about a variety of behavioral difficulties that have a negative effect. The only students motivated by good grades are those already getting good grades.

Harmin, Merrill, *Inspiring Active Learning: A Handbook for Teachers*, 1994, Alexandria, VA Association for Supervision and Curriculum Development. This is a collection of teaching strategies to increase student involvement, group work, confidence, and motivation. The techniques are practical and down-to-earth—I think they will work for anyone, anywhere. Ideas include reducing anxiety, reluctance, and misbehavior. There are hundreds of suggestions for using pairs and student-to-student interaction.

Hart, Leslie A., *The Classroom Disaster*, 1969, Teachers College Press, Columbia University, New York. Written by a layperson, this book questions the basic assumptions of traditional education and attributes problems and ineffectiveness to classroom structures and procedures, claiming the education we desire is not possible in a system that treats students like prison inmates.

Hutchinson, J. N., *Students In The Margins*, 1999, Albany, State University of New York. Hutchinson shows how students can become marginalized from the process of learning when we fail to pay sufficient attention to student's personal stories. Students on the margin do not have the interest, commitment or engagement that would enable them to do quality work. She deals with marginalization via race, gender, and psychosocial factors.

Katz, L.G. and Chard, S.C., *Engaging Children's Minds: The Project Approach*, Ablex Publishing Corp. Norwood, NJ. The project approach takes into account the unevenness of development by enabling children to undertake open-ended tasks along side one another at varying levels of complexity and with equally acceptable outcomes. It lends itself particularly well to teaching children of different ages and ability in one setting. The approach can include the at-risk kids. This book offers all the examples a teacher should need to trigger the imagination and utilize the approach.

Kelly, Earl C., *Education for What Is Real*, 1947, Harper & Row, New York. With a foreword by John Dewey, this book illustrates that children learn by experience, not authority. Kelly challenges 10 myths. His findings are equivalent to a college degree.

Kelly, Earl C., *In Defense of Youth*, 1963, Prentice-Hall, New York. One of my favorite education books; Kelly speaks from his experiences in using humanistic procedures. He argues that, as children became liabilities rather than assets, and communities no longer had places for young people they were forced into the circumstances that are troublesome to schools and society.

Keyes, Ralph, *Is There Life After High School?* 1976. I found that high school is the source of indelible memories that focus on comparison of status, and status comparisons continue long after graduation, in a society shaped fundamentally by high school.

Kohn, Alfie, *The Case Against Standardized Testing*, 2000, Heinemann, Portsmouth, NH. "We've got very interesting studies where teachers do thirty-five or thirty eight weeks of what they think is best for kids, and then they'll give them three weeks of test cramming just before the test. And the kids do just as well as the kids who have forty weeks of test-driven curriculum." "This is corroborated by some research that found a one-hour intensive reading readiness tutorial for young children produced test results equivalent to two years of skills oriented direct instruction."

Mitchell, John G., *Creating User-Friendly Classrooms*, 1995, XL Publications, 4285 Trenton Rd, Clarksville, TN 37040,

(931) 553-2888. Finally a book that practices what it preaches–it is a "user-friendly" book. Cutting through myths and faulty assumptions, the author offers practical, down-to-earth ideas, for virtually every phase of classroom decision making, with explanations and examples that "regular" classroom teachers can and will implement immediately. Dr Mitchell utilizes a well-explained democratic, community, non-reward-punishment classroom. I consider that the teaching strategies espoused by John. Mitchell could create a revolution in education, if they were widely known and distributed.

Nathanson, Donald L., *Shame and Pride*, 1992, W.W. Norton, New York."When our frailties or foibles are exposed before those in whose presence we do not feel safe or loved, this mild humorous embarrassment gives way to the deeper forms of shame like humiliation or mortification."

Polak, Edward, with Bill Page, *Teacher's Aid, A Collection of Ideas and Activities*, Expanded Edition, 1983, Quebec Assn for Children with Learning Disabilities, Montreal Quebec, Canada. Polak and Page present three basic principles: 1. Each child must experience success in the classroom. 2. Each teacher must recognize the uniqueness of each child and accommodate that uniqueness. 3. Each classroom can be mysterious, provocative, energizing, and inviting—it is up to the teacher.

Postman, Neil and Weingartner, Charles, *The School Book*, 1970, Random House, New York. "Relevant Curriculum invites school people to look at what's happening from the students' point of view. This does not mean that one must pander to ephemeral student interest. It does mean that teachers must ask themselves seriously if their reasons for teaching something are based on student needs or their own."

Reeves, Douglas B., *Accountability for Learning: How Teachers and School Leaders Can Take Charge*, 2004, Association for Supervision and Curriculum Development, Alexandria, VA. A surprisingly practical book showing how to create a student-centered accountability system and more importantly, how teachers can and must take charge of their own accountability. Teachers know their effectiveness. They need to record and report their successes.

Reimer, Everett, *School Is Dead, An indictment of the system and a Strategy of Revolution*, 1970, Doubleday & Co, Garden City, NY. "School is the world's largest enterprise; larger than agriculture, industry, or warfare. ...Not only the leaders but their followers are shaped by the school game to play the game of competitive consumption – first to meet and then to surpass the standards of others. Whether the rules are fair or the game worth playing is beside the point."

Rosenberg, Marshall, B., *Life-Enriching Education*, 2003, Puddle-Dancer Press, Encinitas, CA. This book represents a new direction in education (Not because my name is in the acknowledgments and Author's Notes.) because it presents the mutual respect in schools that "everyone talks about but is difficult to find." Dr. Rosenberg was my first mentor, not because he chose to be—it just happened.

Sarason, Seymore B., *And What Do YOU mean By Learning,*

2004, Heinemann, Portsmouth, NH. "Studies clearly indicate that as children go from elementary to middle to high school the value they attach to school learning goes steadily downhill and that is true in suburban and urban schools."

Sizer, Theodore, *The Red Pencil Convictions from experience in education*, 2004, Yale University Press, New Haven, CT. "What primarily sticks with me to this day is fear. What I remember is selective but stark and detailed, retained not for any abiding joy in classics but for the simple reason that Barrell (Latin teacher) terrified me." Sizer also wrote *Horace's Compromise*.

Smith, Frank, The Book of Learning and Forgetting, (1998) Teacher's College Press, New York. The most interesting, thought-provoking book I've ever read (except for any other book by Smith, including *Unspeakable Acts and Unnatural Practices*, 2003. Smith's views are diametrically opposed to conventions, but he does it with irrefutable logic. His credentials include having been a reporter, professor, and editor, a Harvard PhD and publishing 23 books.

Frank Smith, *Insult To Intelligence: The Bureaucratic Invasion Of Our Classrooms*, 1988, Heinemann, Portsmouth, NH. "...programmatic instruction is expected to produce quality education." The myth is based on a misguided theory of learning and the presumption that experts outside the classroom can make better decisions about helping students learn than teachers. The result is the ritualistic teaching of nonsense and instruction with no significant intellectual content. The issue is political, a question of who will control how students are taught.

Bill Page Speaks...
A top educational speaker in the nation for the past 25 years

Super-teacher" a title The Manitoba, Canada Teacher Magazine gave Bill; America's Favorite Classroom Teacher" the name the St Louis Post-Dispatch feature writer gave Bill after following his three-year" research program for middle school troublemakers". Bill Page was so named because of his humorous, entertaining speaking and profound message that gets at the heart of attitude, responsibility--and because of his remarkable success.

Administrators and teachers who hear Bill gain motivation, inspiration, insights, enthusiasm and numerous fresh ideas and strategies for accepting more responsibility for "reaching the hard-to-teach" students. Bill shows how his attitude, determined spirit, and genuine enthusiasm led to dramatic changes in his teaching, in other teachers, administrators and in whole school systems.

Bill Page presents a proven program to change the way administrators interact with teachers. Based on 14 different courses Bill taught at 86 universities including 26 consecutive summers at the University of California at Riverside, San Diego, Irvine, and Santa Barbara, this program content includes;

*Inspiration and motivation for principals to improve teacher effectiveness.
*A perspective on role of administrators in "Closing the Achievement Gap".
*A new and different approach for achieving success with at-risk students
*Strategies building administrators can offer as embedded staff development.
*Ongoing help administrators can offer for use in teachers' daily routines.
*Ideas for all grade levels, all subjects and all students including those at-risk.
*Use of grades, grading, and tests as learning devices not just assessments
*Emphasis on behavior of teachers and students as manifestations of beliefs.
*Better utilization of brain-mind studies and hands-on activities.
*A program guaranteed to change how administrators interact with teachers.
*Change and improvement in attitude and action not just knowledge.

Bill Page speaks on: discipline, motivation, acting-out, failure, disrespect, at-risk characteristics. Speaker, author, Dr Ed Frierson says, *Fw speakrs evk eotòn adpre feg fr a ohanto prov. Hg des t onstetly H i on ofthe best ed tòalspeakrs idrù."*

"I highly recommend Bill Page because what he has to say is immediately implementable and useful for all educators. He does this in a very commonsense, humorous and user-friendly manner."
---Dr. Harry Wong, author of The First Days of School"

Information: www.teacherteacher.com

How To Enjoy
PARENTHOOD
"The Roller coaster Ride Of Your Life"

An album of eight CD's
With 16 half-hour sessions by:
Bill Page and "Dr, Ed" Frierson

Information: www.teacherteacher.com

HOW TO ENJOY YOUR KIDS
INSTEAD OF HASSLING THEM

A program that eliminates the need for
positive reinforcement, bribes, threats,
rewards, punishment, grounding, timeouts,
screaming, and unpleasant stuff parents wind
up doing to kids.
Procedures that can eliminate the frustration,
disappointment, uncertainty, exasperation,
anger, desperation, nagging, and screaming
from the lives of parents.

The Operative Word Is *ENJOY*!

Eight Hours
of Teaching Strategies

Bill Page – Live!

A "How I Do It" Eight Hour Album of CD's

Order On-Line www.teacherteacher.com
or
E-Mail: billpage@bellsouth.net

12 Topics, 8 CD's, In Carrying Pack

1. The Three Most Important Elements of Success
2. The Obligation to Make Classes Interesting
3.   Some Blue Ribbon Ideas—For a change
4. Kids Are Always Motivated, Often To Do Nothing
5. If They Knew What I Knew; They'd Do What I Do
6. Kids Don't Flunk; They Get Flunked
7. I Don't Get Paid To Grade Or Correct Student Papers
8. When Student Failure Is the Teacher's Fault
9. Getting the Kids To Be More Responsible
10. We Teach Individuals or Groups. There Is No Choice
11. How I Eliminated 80% of My Discipline Problems
12. The Only Discipline You'll Ever Need

Satisfaction Guaranteed or
Your Money, including Postage, Back

Bill Page Tells What He Does and How He Does It
You've Never Heard Anything Like It!

Improving Teacher Effectiveness
An Administrators Retreat Program
by Bill Page

Bill Page presents refreshing, an inspirational, humorous, Extremely helpful program to help principals and other administrators help teachers change their attitude, behavior, and effectiveness in their regular daily routines.

Principals through their relationship and embedded continuous, Staff development can improve teacher effectiveness dramatically. The program meshes with other programs and can be implemented Immediately.

The route to educational excellence is via instructional excellence. We cannot expect improved student achievement without a Corresponding improvement in teacher effectiveness.

Once the central office and building administrators spend a half-day or evening with Bill Page, they'll never look at staff development and teacher improvement the same, again

Info: billpage@bellsouth.net.
Visit: www.teacherteacher.com

You'll Never Look at Staff Development the same way again!

Summer Workshops for Teachers

"Getting the New School Year Off To a Great Start"
"Middle School: In a League of Its Own"
"Teaching The Kids Who Cause Trouble in Class"
"Teaching So Kids Will Learn and Remember"

Two Day To Two Week Courses for School Districts

By Bill Page

Since teachers tend to teach the way they themselves were taught; and since they are likely to have had many years of "traditional" schooling, these programs offer alternative teaching strategies that go beyond traditional practices.

One way to help teachers change and improve is to use the summer break to prepare for a new school year with some new ideas and plans. Emphasis is on transition to student centered, student directed, hands-on learning and performance assessment, rubrics, cooperative and authentic learning, etc.

Unlike many professions, teachers have the opportunity to start each year fresh. Beginning with new rules, procedures, fresh ideas, new teaching plans and a great attitude, they can begin immediately the first day and first week establishing a fresh relationship with their students—one that has the potential to grow, develop, and improve as the year progresses.

A ten-page course description may be downloaded at:
www.teacherteacher.com or contact: billlpage@bellsouth.net

Why will teachers be better next year than they were this year?

Order Form

Educational Dynamics
222 Wheeler Avenue,
Nashville TN 37211
615-833-1086
Fax 615.831.0909
billpage@bellsouth
www.teacherteacher.com

❑Send a FREE Newsletter and Bill Page Recent Articles

❑Send Info on Administrator Staff Development Programs

❑Send Info on Bill Page Staff Development Programs

❑Send info on Publications

❑Send Info on Parenting CD Album

❑Send Info on Bill Page LIVE CD Album

❑Send Descriptive Educational Brochures

Orders and Information
615 833 1086

Order on-Line: www.teacherteacher.com

Name_____

Title/Position_____

School/District_____

Address_____

City/State_____Zip_____

Telephone (____)_____Ext_____

Payment Information:

    Personal or School Check Enclosed #_____

    Purchase Order #_____

      Checks payable to Educational Dynamics: